Minnie's Room

How one mother's
active faith
led to redemption
in a place of pain.

Donna Luce

Copyright © 2024-2025 Donna Luce

Published by Dust Jacket Press
Minnie's Room: How One Mother's Active Faith Led Her to Find Redemption in a Place of Pain / Donna Luce

ISBN: 978-1-953285-56-0

All rights reserved. No portion of this publication may be reproduced, stored in a retrieval system, or transmitted in any form or by any means, except for brief quotations in printed reviews, without prior permission of Donna Luce at *donna.luce@hotmail.com*.

Dust Jacket Press
P.O. Box 721243
Oklahoma City, OK 73172

All Scripture quotations not otherwise designated are from the New King James Version®. Copyright © 1982 by Thomas Nelson. Used by permission. All rights reserved.

Permission to quote from the following additional copyrighted versions of the Bible is acknowledged with appreciation:

Amplified Bible (AMP). Copyright © 2015 by The Lockman Foundation, La Habra, CA 90631. All rights reserved.

Holy Bible, New International Version®, NIV® Copyright ©1973, 1978, 1984, 2011 by Biblica, Inc.® Used by permission. All rights reserved worldwide.

Holy Bible, New Living Translation, NLT, copyright © 1996, 2004, 2015 by Tyndale House Foundation. Used by permission of Tyndale House Publishers, Inc., Carol Stream, Illinois 60188. All rights reserved.

Scripture quotation marked KJV is from the King James Version of the Bible.

Cover design by Dominic Masiello with permission of Samantha Christy
Interior design by D.E. West - Dust Jacket Press Creative Services

Printed in the United States of America

To my Domenica, this book is for you so that your story might be told far and wide; that the Lord might use your life, your struggles, and even your death to draw many to Him as they learn of His miracles in your life and mine.

To my husband, Steve, and our other wonderful children, Francesca and Joseph—we are in this together and the Lord continues holding us tightly as we navigate life with one piece of the puzzle missing. You are all steadfast in your faith, and with the help of Jesus, we help hold each other together when another is weak.

To the rest of my family, you have prayed for us, held us tightly, cried with us, and rejoiced with us through it all, and you have helped fill many holes in our broken hearts. We know you are hurting right along with us.

To my prayer warriors, you have been holding up my weary arms as Aaron did for Moses, and I have felt the strength from all your prayers. "A threefold cord is not quickly broken" (Ecclesiastes 4:12 KJV).

*I would have lost heart, unless I had believed that I would
see the goodness of the Lord in the land of the living.*
—Psalm 27:13 NKJV

_____ _____

CONTENTS

Introduction ix

1. History (Her Story) 1
2. Faith versus Trust 23
3. The Character of God: Loving, Faithful, Merciful, Compassionate 31
4. My Prayer Journal 39
5. The Promise 99
6. The Reminder 107
7. His Goodness Is Running after Me 119
8. Hope against All Hope 123
9. Do You Have This Hope? 129
10. My Plea to You from My Heart 135
11. Jesus Was There 141
12. Closing Thoughts 145

Family Gallery 149

Scripture Resource Guide 151

Epilogue 197

Works Cited 199

INTRODUCTION

By your picking up this book, there is a good chance you are a parent in pain for your child. You may be in anguish over a prodigal, mourning the loss of your child, or any number of other sufferings we as parents feel. I suffered many. My prayer is that as you journey with me, you will be encouraged in the wonder of God's awesome miracles and delight in His great mercy and love for us as parents, as we work through some of our deepest sorrows, fears, and shortcomings.

I never intended to write a book, but through the prompting of several friends, many who share some of my struggles with their children, I felt the Lord leading me to bare my heart and my public and private battles, as well as my answers to prayer, in hopes that our story can bring blessing, help, and hope to others. While Minnie's struggles seemed to be rooted in her middle school years, it was the time just before her death when I began to lean hard into the Lord and engage in an active faith. By the time she reached the age of sixteen, we were already struggling with many of her secret sins (she only *thought* they were secret, but the Lord gave us wisdom to find her out). Her struggles included sneaking out of the house at night or sneaking others in, stealing money, lying to family members, and the beginning of her substance abuse. It was years of rebellious behavior that would eventually lead to me finding her lifeless body in her bedroom one horrific November morning, when she succumbed to an accidental fentanyl overdose shortly after her eighteenth birthday.

I don't want you to get caught up in the details about our struggles with Minnie, because her life was more than her struggles. I recorded what I did so you can see the roots of evil that can spring up anywhere in our lives because "your adversary the devil walks about like a roaring lion, seeking whom he may devour" (1 Peter 5:8). We are told to be sober and vigilant, and I believe even more so for the souls of our children.

Yes, there is so much pain and misery here, but I pray that overall you will see not only how God has and continues to carry me through the furnace of affliction but also how His goodness went before my Domenica to ultimately bring her home, where no one could hurt her ever again. Rejoice with me as you see His loving and gentle hands guide, protect, and comfort amid the storm. Understand that although you may not be rejoicing in your current sufferings, God is not finished with your story. Never stop praying and believing. His plan is still unfolding before me, and we may never know the entire story until we are with Him in eternity.

1

HISTORY (HER STORY)

I started grieving for Domenica long before she left this earth. As strong believers in Jesus Christ, having been raised in church and subsequently raising our three children (Francesca, Domenica, and Joseph) in church, my husband, Steve, and I started worrying when we began seeing some changes in our daughter around seventh grade. That's when I started prayer journaling, and that's where my journey from grief to grace began. As I write this, I'm still in the early and agonizing stages of grief, yet somehow I feel that this raw emotion can help other grieving parents, and these thoughts and emotions need to be written.

Domenica ("Minnie") was a joy from the start, bringing so much love and laughter to our family and those around her. Our constant entertainer, wearing all the "spinning skirts" and sparkles, she had a carefree attitude and a special something about her that made everyone around her know she was special in many ways—until the darkness entered and her innocence was stolen by dark, evil forces that she was too young and powerless to fight off. We tried everything as parents to rescue her from this, but the damage was done and the guilt and shame gave way to bad choices, reckless behaviors, and dark mental health issues that tormented her day and night. She eventually told me about the hellish nightmares that plagued her and eventually caused her to lose faith in a God she could not see as loving for all the misery she was in. What she didn't understand is that the verse chosen over her life when we dedicated her to the Lord as a baby was Jeremiah 29:11—*"I know the plans I have for you," declares the Lord, "plans to prosper you and not to harm you, plans to give you hope and a future."* As she got older I continued to remind her of this verse, but her young, damaged, earthly eyes could not see hope or a future.

When I refer to her eyes as "damaged," I mean this in the most severe sense of the word. I had installed a keystroke recorder on the computer, only by the grace of God. Minnie loved watching YouTube videos, first of her favorite rides at Disneyland. Then as she got older she moved to Barbie videos. As YouTube's programing goes, video suggestions are generated automatically at the end of each viewed video. The revolting, demonic powers that govern our Internet thought it would be a good idea to sneak in a vile (but mainstream) video suggestion for my ten-year-old daughter. In her innocence she clicked, which led to a worse suggestion and a worse one after that. Before we knew it, our sweet preteen girl, who loved Jesus and had the joy of the Lord pouring out of her, had developed a full-blown addiction to hardcore pornography before even reaching middle school. Our girl who loved to dance, sing, make funny faces, and cause people to laugh became reclusive, depressed, and moody. Minnie's room, once filled with music and laughter, became her personal prison of her

> *Minnie's room, once filled with music and laughter, became her personal prison.*

actions and her mind. It was the place of violent nightmares, self-mutilation, secret sins, a place she hated but could not escape, and eventually the place where she would take her final breath on earth.

Recently as I shared this story with a friend who had been sexually abused as a child, she told me she learned in therapy that pornography use in children does damage to the same parts of the brain as actual physical abuse does. This makes so much sense to me now, because Minnie had told me in later years that she believed pornography was the root of all her problems. I have since heard from pastors that pornography can open portals to the demonic realm in our lives and should never be touched.

I first noticed the cuts when Minnie was in junior high, although the change in her countenance and disposition began long before that. This is when the journaling began. The fear I felt combined with my inadequacy as a parent to deal with these issues developed into anger as she pulled away more and more. I'm sure many parents can relate to this, especially with teenage daughters, and I look back and constantly question what I could have done differently at this time in her life when she so desperately needed rescuing.

During this period we took her to a Christian counselor, who was lovely and caring but not equipped to handle the depth of what Minnie was going through. However, she assured me that cutting was not a sign of suicidal thoughts but was instead a coping mechanism to deal with whatever pain she was experiencing inside. That at least set my mind more at ease, but it was at this time that I started watching her like a hawk, questioning everything she said and did, and our relationship suffered greatly. This led to so many intense and heated arguments, and I didn't realize that the changes in her were being fueled not only by the dark oppression of her mind but also by the developing mental health concerns that would be slowly discovered over the next several years.

FAITH IN ACTION:
PRAYER

Rejoice always, pray without ceasing, in everything give thanks; for this is the will of God in Christ Jesus for you.
(1 Thessalonians 5:16–18)

Keep on asking, and you will receive what you ask for. Keep on seeking, and you will find. Keep on knocking, and the door will be opened to you.
(Matthew 7:7 NLT)

OCTOBER 23, 2018

God, I don't even know where to start. My heart is breaking for my Minnie. I've seen the transformation in her life from the silly, giggly little girl who made us laugh like crazy to a sad, moody teen who I feel hates me most of the time. The gash on her face and the one on her arm weren't accidents! She doesn't talk to me, and when she does, it's rude and hurts my heart. I heard today on Christian radio that I need to mourn the loss of my little girl. She's gone, and that means the mommy of that little girl needs to be gone too. She needs me to be different for her now, but I don't know who that is. Please, Jesus, show me who I need to be for my Minnie, to help her navigate through these hard years so she can bloom into a beautiful, godly young lady. I still see hints of her heart for You, but it's overshadowed by a darkness that is covering her right now. My heart is broken. Lord, please restore the light and joy in her heart. Help us to get through this time and come out closer than we've ever been. Protect her heart and her mind from all the evil that surrounds her at school each day. I know she will make mistakes, God, but please protect her from making life-altering mistakes. Please show Minnie Your love for her and Your grace and mercy for those secret sins I know she is hiding from me. Show her that she can find healing at the cross. Give her a distaste for sin and this world and a longing for You and Your will for her life. Help her to change those around her instead of being changed by them. God, Minnie is not mine. You lent her to me for a short time. I put her in Your hands, knowing there is only so much I can do and that I need You to do the work I cannot. I know You love her even more than I do, so please work in her life even as I pray.

> *Satan knows our weaknesses and will certainly exploit them.*

[Reading this first journal entry is so difficult. From the beginning, I trusted that the Lord would get her through this. I was so expectant of seeing great miracles in her life.]

Throughout this time she had a boyfriend, and because of the problems she was exhibiting, both his mother and I felt it would be best for them not to be together. He eventually broke up with her, which sent her into a deeper decline, and because he told her it was my fault, this was also the beginning of her anger toward me that she never really let go of for the rest of her life. He also told her I didn't want them together because he wasn't a Christian, which is also why she started questioning her faith during these fragile years. Satan knows our weaknesses and will certainly exploit them.

OCTOBER 29, 2018

My God, my heart is broken. I found definite evidence last night that Minnie is cutting herself. It's hard to even say it or write it because it's one of those things I don't understand. It seems so dark and hopeless, and I'm so worried about her. She has emotional pain so deep that there is nothing I can do, and now it's leaving physical scars so deep they may never heal. Jesus, I cry out to You for my baby! Lead us to the right counselor for her. She needs help that I can't give her. I don't know where all the pain is from. God, forgive me if I've caused it. I'm sure some of it is from me. God, help her to see that she is Your workmanship, Your masterpiece, Your work of art. Let Your voice be louder than the outside voices that tell her she's ugly, not good enough, not worthy of love. Sing over her, shout it if she doesn't hear, embrace her when she feels alone, give her a way out when she is desperate. And please help me to be the mom she needs right now, to love her how she needs to be loved. I need a miracle, God!

FAITH IN ACTION:
ANOINTING OIL

Is anyone among you sick? Let him call for the elders of the church, and let them pray over him, anointing him with oil in the name of the Lord. And the prayer of faith will s ave the sick, and the Lord will raise him up. And if he has committed sins, he will be forgiven.
(James 5:14–15)

They cast out many demons, and anointed with oil many who were sick, and healed them.
(Mark 6:13)

Around this time I knew I needed to anoint her room with oil. In the Old Testament oil was used to sanctify or consecrate priests or to set them apart as holy. In the New Testament we are told in Mark 6:1, "They cast out many demons, and anointed with oil many who were sick, and healed them." James 5:14 tells us, "Is anyone among you sick? Let him call for the elders of the church, and let them pray over him, anointing him with oil in the name of the Lord." So we can conclude that oil is used both for healing and as a symbol of the Holy Spirit. For this reason I anointed everything in our house, and specifically her room, with oil, praying to break strongholds and inviting the Holy Spirit into every inch of our home. I prayed that the Holy Spirit would bring an uncomfortable conviction upon Minnie until she returned to the Lord.

Looking back, I believe this is one reason she grew to hate home. Home was the place where she felt the weight of conviction and the spiritual battle that raged in her. She blamed it on me, but she didn't realize it was the Holy Spirit doing His job to convict and discipline those the Lord loves. And as much as the Lord was tugging on her heart in one direction, Satan was pulling to the same degree, if not harder, in the other direction. I do feel that unseen war played a huge role in her mental health, and the more she pulled away from God, the worse it got because the Good Shepherd will never leave one of His sheep who has strayed.

When Minnie entered high school I was thrilled that she decided to play volleyball, along with Francesca, who was a senior at the same high school. This kept her busy and exercising—two things she greatly needed for her mental health—and we started seeing glimpses of our sweet, fun-loving Minnie. Although it was a struggle, she was even in honors classes and doing well. She was making new friends from the volleyball team and loving her role as the ace server.

Her relationship with Francesca grew deeper because they would drive to school together and get there early. They would sit in the car and talk before school started each day. Minnie would often hang out with Francesca and her friends outside of school, which made her feel special and important. She was going to dances and other school activities and simply getting the most out of her high school experience.

Then COVID-19 hit and everything came to a screeching halt for everyone. At first we made the best of the shutdown, taking walks, camping, lying out in the sun, and doing puzzles; but as the days dragged into weeks, and weeks into months, I saw a fast and definite decline in Minnie's mental health. Joseph was thirteen at the time and also went into a mental tailspin, but it was his strong relationship with Jesus and deep convictions that helped pull him through this time. It was heart-wrenching watching Minnie as she became a recluse, hardly ever venturing out of her room or even her bed. She was sedentary to the extreme sense of the word, and it didn't help that she had braces and was in that dreaded awkward time in every girl's life. No amount of love and concern, words of wisdom, "talks," arguments, threats, or anger did anything to ease the situation.

Although she was happy for her sister, Minnie helplessly watched her best friend slipping away.

I feel what made it extra hard for Minnie was watching Francesca bloom and thrive during this time. School was shut down and her senior year was all but finished, and she had already decided she was going to play volleyball at a local junior college. Francesca was able to enjoy the freedom of spending her days lying out by the pool and taking road trips to anywhere but here. Minnie didn't see her sister (her rock) much during this time.

On one particular road trip to see Grandpa in Texas, Francesca met a young man who lived there. As soon as I learned about him, I knew I would lose my girl to Texas, and I'm sure Minnie knew as well. She did love Francesca's boyfriend very much, and they would often talk or text each other. He treated Minnie like a little sister, and although she was happy for her sister, Minnie helplessly watched her best friend slipping away.

During these long days and nights of COVID-19 solitude, Minnie suddenly began mentioning names of new "friends" and started asking if she could ride her bike to the school or other local places to hang out. That is when my momma's intuition kicked into high gear because I knew something was not right. She would peculiarly "lose cell service" so I couldn't get her location or even get in touch with her. Her lies became more obvious as she had to lie to cover up other lies. She became defensive and angry when we questioned her about anything.

One evening she had some of these new friends over the house, and both my husband and I could see they were not good influences and were dragging her down. (We later learned that one of these boys left a lasting emotional scar on our daughter that contributed so much to her mental health issues, specifically dissociative disorder). After they left we found several empty beer bottles. When we confronted her, she said, "I'm so sorry. I know it was wrong. I didn't have any, but they did." My husband let her know that was *never* going to happen again. We thought she would start making better choices.

Call it naivety, but we believed she was just going through some teenage issues that would get better as she got older. We did not want to micromanage everything because she was the type of person who would purposefully try to break every rule imposed on her. I don't know if this was the right way to parent her or not. There was much prayer for wisdom, but we never really figured it out with Minnie. Francesca and Joseph have always been rule-followers. Rules make them feel structured and safe, and so they thrive in school, home, sports, and anything with authority. Minnie was quite the opposite, which we learned very early on. When she was only in third grade she got into trouble at school and was sent home with a note for me to sign. Instead of giving me the note and confessing, she concocted a plan. She told me how much she loved my signature, asking if I could sign my name for her on a paper. She used that and forged my signature on her discipline slip! She was, we learned over the years, a master manipulator, which just made our relationship so much harder because we learned we could not trust anything Minnie told us. She especially knew how to get to me. Steve was often wise to her and tried to tell me, but it was hard for me to believe my baby could deceive me so badly.

In the summer of 2020 we planned our long motor home road trip, as had been our tradition for years. It was always the most special time of games, laughter, and memories, and we all looked forward to it every year as a time to reconnect and grow closer. This year was different. Francesca had to do her volleyball workouts each day, so she stayed home while the rest of us left for three weeks. Driving away from my girl was so difficult, and Minnie and I both cried, but the magic of the road soon had the rest of us anticipating the upcoming weeks of fun together. It was this three-week trip that strengthened and solidified Minnie and Joseph's relationship. From this moment on they had an unbreakable bond, and Minnie became not only his big sister but also his cheerleader and protector as well. I am also a middle child, and I can say I cherish my role because my bond with both of my siblings has meant all the difference in my life. Minnie was blessed with the same, having both an older sister and a younger brother as her best friends.

Minnie's sophomore year began still on lockdown, and her mental health remained poor but steady because we got her started on Lexapro to help take the edge off. It appeared at first to be helping slightly, then on Easter Sunday 2021 as Steve went outside to tend to his Easter brisket in the early hours of the morning, he realized the back door was open. He woke me up, and we quietly crept down the hall with flashlights and weapons to protect our children. We had our motorhome parked outside, and Steve saw that the door was cracked open and one of our bikes was missing. We immediately called the police, and they threw open the door to the motor home with guns raised—only to find Minnie asleep in her bunk! She had taken the bike on a joyride to God-knows-where, and then she went into the motor home to sleep.

You would think having the police point guns at her head would have straightened her out. If it was merely defiance then maybe this would have helped, but as time went on we realized we were dealing with deep-seated and unfathomable mental health issues, as well as (I am convinced) heavy demonic oppression that she could not escape.

> *This began her biggest decline away from Jesus and from reality.*

After school reopened in April 2021, Minnie began finding herself again and started working out and getting in shape—and she asked me to work out with her. I loved that time with her, and I feel that our relationship had started mending. However, one Sunday in May I was called out of the church service to come pick up Minnie because she had left the high school Sunday School class and was having a panic attack in the church restroom. This began her biggest decline away from Jesus and from reality. She confided in me that she felt disassociated from life; in other words, she had a loss of connection between reality, behavior, identity, and even memory. It causes you to take reckless risks because nothing feels real. (We later learned that this is also a symptom of borderline personality disorder, which she would eventually be diagnosed with shortly before her death).

Nevertheless, she was happy to be back at school and enjoying her friends again, although she never went back to playing volleyball. We also took as many family vacations as we could, including our annual motor home summer road trip, this time as an entire family. Minnie was always happiest when we were traveling, and oh, how she made us laugh!

When we returned from summer vacation, Minnie told me that a certain boy from school had asked her out. I dropped her off at the movies, where I got to meet him, and he seemed like a very nice and respectful young man. They started hanging out and he would often come for dinner; he was easy to talk to and appeared to like Minnie a lot. She seemed to be breaking free of some of her past.

Only one month after she started seeing him, I happened to check our surveillance cameras one morning and saw Minnie sneaking her boyfriend into the house very late one night. What ensued was a huge blowout argument, and both his parents and Steve and I kept them apart indefinitely.

Adjusting from the breakup and with nothing to occupy her time, Minnie decided to pour herself into working out once again, and she asked me to join her. During one of our workouts I noticed she had a large bandage on her forearm. When I pressed her about it, she got angry and ran to her room. I knew the cutting had started again, so I went to talk with her about it. I told her I needed to see it to gauge how bad it was, but she wouldn't show me. It turned into an impassioned argument and she became enraged when I told her that if she didn't show me I would need to call someone to come help for her safety. She adamantly refused.

That was the first night (of many more in the coming years) when I didn't sleep, full of fear that I was losing her. The next morning I knew she couldn't stay home alone because of her fragile mental state (she would not even respond to me), but I also had to leave the house for some business. I called her best friend's mom, whom Minnie adored, and she was able to at last get through to her. She came and helped her pack a few things and took Minnie to stay with them for a while until things could settle down. This was September 24, 2021, the first time Minnie left home without us, and it was also the first of many times I would journal, "I have nothing left." It was also when prayer, fasting, and worship became the bread that sustained me daily over the journey I was on.

FAITH IN ACTION:
FASTING

We fasted and petitioned our God about this,
and he answered our prayer.
(Ezra 8:23)

When I heard these things, I sat down and wept. For some days
I mourned and fasted and prayed before the God of heaven.
(Nehemiah 1:4)

He said to them, "This kind can come out by
nothing but prayer and fasting."
(Mark 9:29)

In the Old Testament it appears that fasting with prayer had to do with a sense of need and dependence, and/or of abject helplessness in the face of actual or anticipated calamity. Prayer and fasting are combined in the Old Testament in times of mourning, repentance, and/or deep spiritual need. (*gotquestions.org*)

Matthew 17 tells of an account when the disciples were unable to cast out a demon from a boy. Jesus answered them in verse 21, "This kind does not go out except by prayer and fasting," indicating that fasting is needed in the most critical situations, perhaps as a weapon in our spiritual warfare.

This is when the Lord really started speaking to me from His Word. Little did I know He was filling me with His promises to anchor me for the storm that would hit. I thought these were all promises that would be answers to my prayers for her salvation and deliverance.

MY JOURNAL ENTRY FROM SEPTEMBER 28, 2021:

I praise You for the victory You have already won! Now I just get to watch *how* You will do it—and You *will* do it, Lord—in ways I could never imagine and way better than my own futile attempts. You have already won and now You are just fitting all the pieces together. Healing! Restoration! Salvation! The victory is Yours!

I had no idea when I wrote those words just how profound they would turn out to be.

FAITH IN ACTION:
READING GOD'S WORD

All Scripture is inspired by God and is useful to teach us what is true and to make us realize what is wrong in our lives. It corrects us when we are wrong and teaches us to do what is right. God uses it to prepare and equip his people to do every good work.
(2 Timothy 3:16–17 NLT)

Your word is a lamp to my feet and a light to my path.
(Psalm 119:105)

The word of God is alive and powerful. It is sharper than the sharpest two-edged sword, cutting between soul and spirit, between joint and marrow. It exposes our innermost thoughts and desires.
(Hebrews 4:12 NLT)

I recorded an early example of how the Lord spoke to me, written in my journal on October 18, 2021:

How do I know God is good and He hears me? He speaks! I sat down to read the Bible and Steve texted me a verse to read, Proverbs 21:30: "There is no wisdom or understanding or counsel against the Lord." I read it and I started praying for Minnie, my usual prayer that I would see her salvation, and I reminded God of His promises. I asked Him for wisdom and questioned if I was doing the right things for my kids. I glanced down at my open Word, and there in orange highlighter was Proverbs 22:6: "Train up a child in the way he should go, and when he is old he will not depart from it." Steve had to send me the prior verse today so God could speak His promise to me again! I *will* see her salvation!

In mid-2020 I started listening online to J. D. Farag, a pastor in Hawaii. His signature sendoff at the end of his weekly prophecy updates is a "But God" testimony, taken from Genesis 50:20: *You meant it for evil, but God meant it for good* [many people stop here, but the verse goes on] *and for the salvation of many* (paraphrased). So in December 2021 I started praying that what was meant for evil in Minnie's life, God would use for her good *and* for the salvation of many. That day I named many people specifically and began praying for their salvation. I prayed, "Use this—use her—to increase Your kingdom." Week after week I would listen to these "But God" testimonies, and I kept praying that God would give me my own "But God" testimony someday that I could share.

In her book *Suffering Is Never for Nothing* Elisabeth Elliot wrote, "When I hear a preacher say, 'What you need is a miracle,' I want to say, 'I might think that's what I need, but very often my prayers are really asking for stones. And what God wants to give me is bread, something that will not only feed myself but feed the world as well'" (Elliot 95). As I continue sharing my story, you will see how God provided bread for me, and I pray He will continue to use me to feed those around me.

I don't want to give the impression, even for a second, that I have been this amazing pillar of constant faith. Quite the contrary! I've had to quote to myself almost daily James 1:6: "**When you ask, you must believe and not doubt,** *because the one who doubts is like a wave of the sea, blown and tossed by the wind"* (NIV, emphasis added). One such journal entry shows this tossing back and forth, and I share this, and others in this book, to show that you are not alone!

JANUARY 15, 2022

Broken, crying, heavy-hearted, questioning, asking, seeking, tormented, uneasy, unsettled, burdened, shattered, overwhelmed, distressed . . . Yet . . . remembering, trusting, praying, believing, praising, thanking, convinced, certain, having faith, assured, undoubting, unwavering, steadfast, confident, expecting—*because I know* the God I serve is mighty and able and that He who promised is faithful (Hebrews 10:23). Circumstances don't change who He is.

And again a few days later;

I'm torn between
Holding on and letting go,
Worry and worship,
Fear and faith,
Pacing and praying;
but then I remember that You do not allow
anything to happen to us that is not both for our
benefit and for Your glory.
Waiting, expecting to see what You will do
and how You will do it . . .
knowing You will do it . . .
praising and thanking You because the battle
is already won . . .
because You promised!

What had happened to make me cry out in distress? In the middle of the night I was awakened by someone in the bathroom. It was Minnie throwing up uncontrollably. I couldn't figure out what was wrong until I found a large bottle of vodka half gone. She had sat in the prison of her room for hours drinking and drinking until, thank God, she started throwing it all up.

How could I pray those prayers during a time of desperation? It is because I had pressed in increasingly more deeply with God, reading His precious words to me for hours daily, studying His promises and praying them back to Him, learning all His names revealed by Him and declared about Him. So even though my eye saw the destruction all around me, when I would sit in His presence I would see the *truth* of who He is. It was His goodness that led me to Psalm 40:1–3 on the 29th of January 2022, and it was this passage that I prayed would be Minnie's "But God" testimony:

The Lord began working on me as I sought Him for help with her.

> I waited patiently for the Lord;
> And He inclined to me,
> And heard my cry.
> He also brought me up out of a horrible pit,
> Out of the miry clay,
> And set my feet upon a rock,
> And established my steps.
> He has put a new song in my mouth—
> Praise to our God;
> Many will see it and fear,
> And will trust in the Lord.

FAITH IN ACTION:
MEDITATING ON AND EXAMINING GOD'S WORD

Tune your ears to wisdom, and concentrate on understanding. Cry out for insight, and ask for understanding. Search for them as you would for silver; seek them like hidden treasures. Then you will understand what it means to fear the Lord, and you will gain knowledge of God.
(Proverbs 2:2–5 NLT)

Study this Book of Instruction continually. Meditate on it day and night so you will be sure to obey everything written in it. Only then will you prosper and succeed in all you do.
(Joshua 1:8 NLT)

Study and do your best to present yourself to God approved, a workman [tested by trial] who has no reason to be ashamed, accurately handling and skillfully teaching the word of truth.
(2 Timothy 2:15 AMP)

Early in this journey with Minnie I picked up an old devotional that had helped me through another desperate time in my life—*Streams in the Desert,* by L. B. Cowman. I also added *Faith's Checkbook,* by Charles Spurgeon. I still read these daily because, along with the Bible, they make a beautiful trifecta for anyone going through a relentless and impossible trial. There were days I would be praying in desperation, face between my knees, asking God for an answer for something specific or a word I needed for that moment, and I would open my Bible or one of those books, and the Scripture reading for the day was like God calling down from heaven speaking to me. It's like what David prayed in Psalm 40:1: "I waited patiently for the Lord; and He inclined to me, and heard my cry." I picture the great God of the universe bending closely with His hand cupping His ear to listen intently as I cry out to Him. That is my very personal God, who loves me and cares. That is my God, of whom the psalmist wrote, "You keep track of all my sorrows. You have collected all my tears in your bottle. You have recorded each one in your book" (Psalm 56:8 NLT).

Minnie's heart was always toward helping others. She was a true empath. She worked as a server at an assisted living facility, and she had such a tender spot for the elderly, probably because of all the special time she spent with her grandparents throughout her life. She would come home with stories about the residents, often retelling them through tears. She loved sitting with them, listening to their stories, and just making them feel important. Her ultimate goal was to be a firefighter, but when her harmful decisions robbed her health, she began looking for other ways to help people. Because of her love for true crime stories and always cheering for the underdog, she had set her sights on a career in criminal justice and was set to begin classes in just a month. Empathy was her gift from God, but sadly, it led her to connect with others (particularly guys) who dragged her down.

Minnie went on to make about every bad choice someone could make. She ran away from home several times, the last time on her eighteenth birthday, when she lived on the street with her boyfriend. In moments of clarity Minnie told us she knew he was evil because there were times she saw complete darkness in his eyes. (I also believe that was the stronghold he had over her—the fact that she could not escape him no matter how much she wanted to and tried.) She also ended up in the hospital for numerous reasons, all caused by her own bad decisions.

One of her most ruthless struggles, which was in reality another addiction, was anorexia and bulimia. Many of the boys she associated with were not only physically but also mentally abusive, and they constantly, hatefully criticized her for her developing looks and body. We tried to attack this disorder with therapy, but in June 2023 we finally had to admit her to a facility because her eating disorder had nearly taken her life. Her medical evaluation checked her in at ninety-six pounds.

This eating disorder robbed her of two jobs she positively loved, plus it prevented her from attending the last several months of her senior year of high school and even attending her own high school graduation. I tried so hard to help her through it, but instead, it incited anger in her, which she directed at me, although I knew in reality she was angry with herself. But I want you to know that through it all, our relationship grew deeper and deeper as I learned to rely on the Lord for guidance and less on myself and my natural inclination to just get embittered and angry. In the past, as my frustration with her rebellion and self-harm grew, we would get in heated and very loud arguments that left us both feeling destitute as we helplessly watched our relationship fall apart. But the Lord began working on *me* as I sought Him for help with her, and as time went on, she and I would have long meaningful conversations about her future and the beautiful plans she had, and I often reminded her of the verse spoken over her at her baby dedication.

She would tell me how she hated the things she was doing and wanted so badly to be free of it all. She shared with me her torments as she would try sleeping at night and couldn't; the torments that started when she was young; the torments that Satan would scare her with and cause her to doubt who her Jesus was; the torments that caused her to disassociate with life so she had to always search for the next high (either good or bad) just to feel anything; the torments that would eventually lead to her death, not knowing that the drugs she took to cope with life would be what Satan would use to take her life—*but God.*

Let me first tell you how the Lord worked in my life to constantly draw me in to Him more and more deeply. Think about how Jesus was always surrounded by a multitude, but often He would take the twelve disciples and pull only them aside to teach them deeper truths about Himself that the multitude could not understand. Then there were times, as on the Mount of Transfiguration (Matthew 17; Mark 9; Luke 9) and in the Garden of Gethsemane (Matthew 26; Mark 14; Luke 22; John 18) when Jesus called His closest friends—Peter, James, and John—to go deeper with Him than with all the rest. He revealed great and awesome truths about Himself to them, yet He also required the most from them (as when He scolded them for sleeping instead of praying with Him in the garden).

Jesus draws us to deeper levels of communion with Him so we can hear Him speaking "face to face, as a man speaks with his friend" (Exodus 33:11). I do feel that these years of darkness and trials with Minnie was Jesus pulling me more deeply, more closely, and more intimately with Him. He honestly is still working in my life, transforming me in the fire. When the Hebrew young men were thrown into the fire (Daniel 3), Jesus was there with them and they came out unsinged, yet the ropes that bound them had burned off. God is burning off so many things that have bound me in my life, and yes, Jesus has been there in this fire with me all along.

How did He call me more deeply into Himself? It was through prayer—my constant attitude of prayer all day, every day, innumerable days of fasting and praying, and those moments of face flat on the floor crying out in anguished prayer! I read in *Streams in the Desert,* "Pray until what you pray for has been accomplished or until you have complete assurance in your heart that it will be. . . . Prayer is not only calling on God but is also a battle with Satan" (Cowman 185). Don't ever give up praying. It is our lifeline to our amazing God!

2

FAITH VERSUS TRUST

When Minnie's downhill spiral became more aggressive in 2021, the Lord almost audibly gave me the promise "I would have lost heart, *unless I had believed* that I would see the goodness of the Lord in the land of the living" (Psalm 27:13, emphasis added). I added the emphasis here because this is the key to this verse. The Scriptures are replete with verse after verse about faith; in fact, the entire chapter of Hebrews 11 is about the heroes of faith who have gone before us. But what is faith and is it the same thing as trust?

> If your faith rests in your idea of how God is supposed to answer your prayers, your idea of heaven here on earth or pie in the sky or whatever, then that kind of faith is very shaky and is bound to be demolished when the storms of life hit it. But if your faith rests on the character of Him who is the eternal I AM,

then that kind of faith is rugged and will endure. (Elliot 93)

Let's see what the Bible says about faith and hope as a starting point. Hebrews 11:1 tells us, "Now faith is confidence in what we hope for and assurance about what we do not see" (NIV). This is a great starting point, but we need to break it down a bit more. The Bible says, "We live by faith, not by sight" (2 Corinthians 5:7 NIV). But what is faith? We need to look at Abraham to get a good picture of what true faith is. Romans 4:18–21 reveals,

> Against all hope, Abraham in hope believed and so became the father of many nations, just as it had been said to him, "So shall your offspring be." Without weakening in his faith, he faced the fact that his body was as good as dead—since he was about a hundred years old—and that Sarah's womb was also dead. Yet he did not waver through unbelief regarding the promise of God, but was strengthened in his faith and gave glory to God, being fully persuaded that God had power to do what he had promised. (NIV)

The key is verse 21: *being fully persuaded that God had power to do what He had promised.* Abraham was ninety-nine and his wife, Sarah, was well past child-bearing years, yet the Lord promised him descendants as numerous as the sands of the sea. The Lord promised Abraham land in faraway Canaan, and He promised him that the whole world would be blessed because of him (Genesis 17). Nothing in Abraham's current situation would cause him to believe, but he served the God

Donna, against all hope, in hope believed.

of the impossible (Jeremiah 32:27). In fact, it would be twenty-five years before Abraham would even begin seeing the fruit of this promise, yet he never wavered regarding the promise.

How do you define this hope? Is it believing that a certain circumstance will work out in our favor? Absolutely not! That is merely optimism, but hope is much different. The Greek word for *hope* found here in Romans 4:18 is *elpis,* which means "to anticipate, to expect what is *sure*, to trust, or to have confidence." So when "against all hope, Abraham in hope believed," that means the circumstances he saw with his earthly eyes could never overshadow his trust or confidence about what he knew were the *sure* promises of God.

Our faith, like hope, is not just having positive beliefs, in the sense that *Oh, I hope I get this or that for Christmas,* or *I hope I get this job,* and so on. True faith is when everything around us is falling apart and there is no possible way out; we *still* have the assurance that God will do what He promised.

Why? Here is the key, so don't miss this—our faith and hope are not based on us and how much we believe or how hard we pray. Our faith is based on God and who He says He is. It is when I began recognizing who He is and who I am not, that my faith *in* God became trust that He *would* do what He said He would do. The Lord tells us so much about who He is in His Word to us. We can know all about His character, and based on what we *know*, we not only can have faith in Him but we can also trust Him *against all hope*. I started saying daily as a reminder, "Donna, against all hope, in hope believed." Scripture is there for us personally. The Lord wrote it for each one of us individually so that we can insert our names into those promises.

Let me put it like this: my daddy is the most honest man I know, and not only that, but he is also the most loving, encouraging, and self-sacrificing person I know, the one who would always give up his jacket or his last bite of food to one of his family. He loves every one of his kids and grandkids (and of course my mom) with every ounce of who he is. So knowing who he is, because he has shown me time after time who he is and has never wavered from that, if he were to promise something to me, I could trust that he would follow through on that promise. His promise to me is as good as done because he said it.

If my earthly daddy can be trusted with his word, then I know without a doubt that my heavenly Father will never go back on His promises. "If you then, being evil, know how to give good gifts to your children, how much more will your Father who is in heaven give good things to those who ask Him!" (Matthew 7:11). It is when we come to this point that our faith becomes trust. We can trust the one in whom we have faith because of who He is. Faith that is resolute and unshakable will always prove God's faithfulness!

A. B. Simpson said, "Allow God time to work and He surely will. Then the very trials that threatened to overcome you with discouragement and disaster will become God's opportunity to reveal His grace and glory in your life, in ways you have never known before." He went on to say, "Living a life of faith often requires us to leave things alone. If we have completely entrusted something to God, we must keep our hands off it. He can guard it better than we can, and He does not need our help. . . . And He will work at the perfect moment, if we will completely trust Him to work in His own way and in His own time" (quoted in Cowman 210, 262). This tells me again that the work God performed in Minnie's life (and death) was Him working in His own way, at His perfect moment.

As Charles H. Spurgeon wrote, "Continue to wait in hope, for although the promise may linger, it will never come too late" (quoted in Cowman 381). And F. B. Meyer wrote, "God may keep you waiting, but He will always remember His promise and will appear in time to fulfill His sacred Word that cannot be broken" (quoted in Cowman 387). And we know that the Lord has timeless knowledge and unlimited resources to bring about His promises. After all, it would not be a miracle if the situation were not desperate, if it could be worked out by human understanding.

FAITH IN ACTION:

PRAISE AND WORSHIP

Then Job arose, tore his robe, and shaved his head;
and he fell to the ground and worshiped. And he said:
"Naked I came from my mother's womb, and naked shall
I return there. The Lord gave, and the Lord has taken away;
Blessed be the name of the Lord."
(Job 1:20–21)

O Lord, You are my God. I will exalt You,
I will praise Your name, for You have done wonderful things;
Your counsels of old are faithfulness and truth.
(Isaiah 25:1)

Why am I discouraged? Why is my heart so sad? I will put my hope
in God! I will praise him again—my Savior and my God!
(Psalm 42:11 NLT)

I'll be honest—I struggled so much with *knowing* who God is and *believing* that He would actually answer my urgent prayer for Minnie. I so desperately wanted to write her a "come to Jesus" letter in case I died or was raptured, but I finally determined in my heart that if I wrote this letter it would mean I didn't trust God to hold true to His Psalm 27:13 promise to me. So I determined on October 16, 2022, and I wrote in the margin of my journal, that I would not write that letter because I believed God would do what

He promised! Here is the devotional from that day that brought me to this point:

> We should never give ourselves the freedom to doubt God or His eternal love and faithfulness toward us in everything. . . . It is very easy to fall into the habit of doubting, worrying, wondering if God has forsaken us, and thinking that after all we have been through, our hopes are going to end in failure. . . . Let us rejoice by faith, by firm determination, and by simply regarding it as true, and we will find that God will make it real to us. The devil has two very masterful tricks. The first is to tempt us to become discouraged, for then we are defeated and of no service to others. . . . The other is to tempt us to doubt, thereby breaking the bond of faith that unites us with the Father. (quoted in Cowman 390)

As Charles Gallaudet Trumbull stated, "God is going to test me with delays, and along with the delays will come suffering. Yet through it all God's promise stands" (quoted in Cowman 393). With this firm foundation comes the true peace of God "which surpasses all understanding" (Philippians 4:7).

Janet Erskine Stuart said, "Joy is not the absence of suffering but the presence of God" (quoted in Elliot 14). Does the presence of God change the fact that I lost my beautiful daughter? No, but it did cause me to run into the arms of the only one who could give me comfort,

> *The education of suffering has taught me indispensable truths about my Lord.*

hope, and even joy. This long and bitter trial has brought me into an intimacy with the Lord that I could have never known without the medium of suffering. It has caused me to truly grasp the concept of God as "I AM"; not "I Was" or "I Will Be"—but "I AM"! He is everything I have ever needed, anything I need at this very moment, and everything I will ever need for tomorrow. The education of suffering has taught me indispensable truths about my Lord. C. S. Lewis wrote, "God whispers to us in our pleasures, speaks in our conscience, but shouts in our pain; it is His megaphone to rouse a deaf world" (Lewis 83).

As in the poem "Footprints in the Sand," I have often felt that God is farthest away when I have needed Him most. However, looking back, I see that it has been those times when He has been carrying me. Psalm 142:3 says, "When my spirit was overwhelmed within me, then You knew my path." And 1 Kings 8:56 assures us that "Not one word has failed of all the good promises He gave" (NIV).

As Elisabeth Elliot stated in *Suffering Is Never for Nothing,* "Out of the deepest waters and the hottest fires have come the deepest things that I know about God" (Elliot 9). This echoes the psalmist when he sang, "Out of the depths I have cried to You, O Lord; Lord, hear my voice! . . . I wait for the Lord, my soul waits, and in His word I do hope" (Psalm 130: 1–2, 5).

Our faith must be grounded on God's character. "He is either God, or He's not. I am either held in the Everlasting Arms, or I'm at the mercy of chance" (Elliot 27). I once heard a saying that I've kept close during this time: "God is not who I *think* He is; God is who He *says* He is." So let us look at who He is. This is such a short list, and I implore you to add to this as you study His Word.

3

THE CHARACTER OF GOD:
LOVING, FAITHFUL, MERCIFUL, COMPASSIONATE

FAITH IN ACTION:

INTERCESSION

*Pray in the Spirit at all times and on every occasion.
Stay alert and be persistent in your prayers for all believers everywhere.*
(Ephesians 6:18 NLT)

We always thank God for all of you and pray for you constantly.
(1 Thessalonians 1:2)

The verses quoted previously, and so many more, bring me much comfort, knowing that God is not some cosmic bully waiting to squash anyone who sins—no! Is the Lord sending trials merely to test our faith, so that we fear the next shoe falling, so to speak? Absolutely not! Anything He allows or sends our way is also meant for our good and His glory. He is so loving, merciful, and compassionate, that even when His people turned on Him again and again—when they would cry out for help He would turn from His anger and come to their rescue. He longs to be merciful to us, to save us from wrath!

What is mercy? Let us first take a look at the definition of *grace*. Grace is God's unmerited favor; in other words, it's getting the good that we *don't* deserve. It's God's abundant blessings for this life and His unfathomable riches for eternity. So how is this different than mercy? Mercy is *not* getting what we *do* deserve; namely, the punishment for our sins, which God instead poured out on Jesus!

Compassion is the basis for mercy. It's God's tenderness and empathy toward us that cause Him to be merciful. Because God is love, compassion is the heart of all He does.

What about faithfulness? This is God's steadfast or immovable love and trustworthiness. Wow! What a great God!

Lamentations 3:22–23 is such a beautiful picture that speaks of God's love, mercy, and faithfulness because they do go hand in hand. "Because of the Lord's great love we are not consumed, for his compassions never fail. They are new every morning; great is your faithfulness" (NIV).

God's faithfulness is referenced time and time again throughout the span of the Bible:

First Thessalonians 5:24 says, "He who calls you *is* faithful, who also will do *it*" (emphasis added)

Hebrews 10:23 urges us, "Let us hold unswervingly to the hope we profess, for He who promised is faithful" (NIV).

Deuteronomy 7:9 says, "Therefore know that the Lord your God, He *is* God, the faithful God who keeps covenant and mercy for a thousand generations with those who love Him and keep His commandments."

Psalm 145:17 tells us, "The Lord is righteous in all his ways and faithful in all He does" (NIV).

Isaiah 30:18 states, "Therefore the Lord will wait, that He may be gracious to you; And therefore He will be exalted, that He may have mercy on you. For the Lord is a God of justice; Blessed are all those who wait for Him."

James 5:11 says, "The Lord is very compassionate and merciful."

Lamentations 3:32 notes, "Though He causes grief, yet He will show compassion according to the multitude of His mercies."

Psalm 116:5 tells us, "Gracious is the Lord, and righteous; yes, our God is merciful."

"We do not know what to do, but our eyes are on you."

Psalm 145:9 states, "The Lord is good to all; He has compassion on all he has made" (NIV).

Romans 9:15–16 reminds us, "For He says to Moses, 'I will have mercy on whomever I will have mercy, and I will have compassion on whomever I will have compassion.' So then it is not of him who wills, nor of him who runs, but of God who shows mercy."

I have found the most beautiful, complete picture of our Lord in Psalm 103. Read it and let this wash over your soul as you see the heart of the Father toward His children:

> Bless the Lord, O my soul;And all that is within
>   me, bless His holy name!
> Bless the Lord, O my soul,
> And forget not all His benefits:
> Who forgives all your iniquities,
> Who heals all your diseases,
> Who redeems your life from destruction,
> Who crowns you with lovingkindness and tender mercies,
> Who satisfies your mouth with good things,
> So that your youth is renewed like the eagle's.
> The Lord executes righteousness

And justice for all who are oppressed.
He made known His ways to Moses,
His acts to the children of Israel.
The Lord is merciful and gracious,
Slow to anger, and abounding in mercy.
He will not always strive with us,
Nor will He keep His anger forever.
He has not dealt with us according to our sins,
Nor punished us according to our iniquities.
For as the heavens are high above the earth,
So great is His mercy toward those who fear Him;
As far as the east is from the west,
So far has He removed our transgressions from us.
As a father pities his children,
So the Lord pities those who fear Him.
For He knows our frame;
He remembers that we are dust.
As for man, his days are like grass;
As a flower of the field, so he flourishes.
For the wind passes over it, and it is gone,
And its place remembers it no more.
But the mercy of the Lord is from everlasting
    to everlasting
On those who fear Him,
And His righteousness to children's children,
To such as keep His covenant,
And to those who remember His commandments
    to do them.
The Lord has established His throne in heaven,
And His kingdom rules over all.
Bless the Lord, you His angels,
Who excel in strength, who do His word,
Heeding the voice of His word.

Bless the Lord, all you His hosts,
You ministers of His, who do His pleasure.
Bless the Lord, all His works,
In all places of His dominion.
Bless the Lord, O my soul!

PROMISE KEEPER

Now that we know who God is, let's take a look at some of His promises for parents struggling with their children who are either unbelieving, caught in a web of sin, or struggling with other issues like depression and other mental health problems. When we are struggling, the Lord gives us help from various places and speaks to us from others. My sister sent me a blog post from *Revive Our Hearts,* written by Jenny Walsh (Walsh 2019). I printed it out and kept it in my journal, where I read it every single day for over a year. I pray these excerpts speak to you as much as they did to me. I've added some of my own sentiments to it as well.

> One day during his senior year in high school, my son left the house taking a car and money withdrawn from his savings account. He sent me this text: "Don't try to find me." We knew he had depression and was smoking marijuana, but now we realized that he was an addict using all kinds of drugs. I was frantic. [*I read this blog even before Minnie took off on her eighteenth birthday. I had no idea just how much I would relate to this momma.*] Have you ever thought you were losing the spiritual battle over your child as one thing after another goes wrong even as you pray with all your heart? Do you have a child who is in trouble with drugs, alcohol, sexual promiscuity or sexual identity

issues, eating disorders, self-injuring, depression, suicide attempts or other mental health disorders, legal troubles, or behavioral issues? [*Whoa! Check the boxes here—this is when this blog grabbed me and I knew the Lord was speaking to me through it.*]

Continuing to pray boldly when circumstances are getting worse and worse is a struggle. I know. I have been there. [*This spoke volumes to me! This is the faith-versus-trust issue I talked about.*].

In her blog Walsh made several points about *how* to pray for our children.

1. PRAY WITH INCREASING FAITH, NOT FEAR.

She highlighted 2 Chronicles 20:12, 15, 17, a passage I've read over many times, but now it stood out in bold to me. "We do not know what to do, but our eyes are on you. . . . This is what the Lord says to you: 'Do not be afraid or discouraged because of this vast army. For the battle is not yours, but God's. . . . You will not have to fight this battle. Take up your positions; stand firm and see the deliverance the Lord will give you'" (NIV). I realized that I was trying to, in a sense, micromanage the Lord with my prayers; praying for every little detail instead of saying, "I don't know what to do, but my eyes are on You." I saw the "vast army" that was coming against my girl, and I had no possible way to victory for her until the Lord showed me here that it was not my battle; *He* would fight for her. My position was on my knees in prayer, and He alone would deliver.

2. PRAY BY RELEASING YOUR PRODIGAL.

Have you ever just groaned before the Lord, flat on your face, weeping and not even being able to find the words to pray? Walsh reminded me of Romans 8:26: "Likewise the Spirit also helps in our weaknesses. For we do not know what we should pray for as we ought, but the Spirit Himself makes intercession for us with groanings which cannot be uttered," and again in Romans 8:34 she pointed out that Jesus sits right next to God the Father and intercedes for us. Wow! The thought of Jesus praying for me, for my family, directly to the Father is remarkably overwhelming. Revelation 5:8 tells about golden bowls of incense, which are before the Lamb (Jesus) in heaven. This incense is the prayers of the saints, the believers throughout history, and it is eternally burning before Jesus. He hears our prayers, and when we do not know how to pray, He intercedes for us. There is no better place to lay our children than at the feet of the one who knows what is eternally best for them.

3. PRAY PERSISTENTLY THROUGH HOPE IN CHRIST.

Praying persistently through hope is praying *bold* prayers. Walsh encouraged praying that the Lord would help me let go of my shame and guilt. There is always plenty of guilt as a parent. Did I raise them right? What did I do wrong? What could I have done differently? She inspired me to pray for faith like the faith of those described in Hebrews 11. This was the big one for me. Could I pray that prayer I knew I needed to pray, the prayer every parent dreads—the prayer in which you finally release your child to God to do what He needs to do to accomplish His plan? She reminded me that "my hope is only in Christ, not in treatment centers, doctors, choices I make or my family makes, circumstances, or anything else. My hope is *only* in Christ." This hit me hard. I was always searching for the next form of help for Minnie; another therapist, another medication, another treatment center, and so on. Sometimes we become so caught up in trying hard that we forget that, at the end of the day, our help comes only from the Lord.

Walsh concluded, "Don't give up praying, even when it seems like the battle is being lost. May the Lord encourage you and show you how He would have you pray and surrender your children to Him. God loves them more than you ever could." That became the end of my every prayer; *God, You love Minnie more than I ever could.*

Getting back to bold prayers, every time I would pray I would remind God that my will was indeed His will because I knew His will was that Minnie would come back to Him. However, I would continue to try to direct God on how that should look. She would finally come to her senses, like in the parable of the prodigal son (Luke 15:17), ask me to pray with her, and she would want to be baptized, and we would live happily ever after. Finally, I was the one who came to *my* senses. I had to humble myself under God's mighty hand and admit that only *He* knew how to rescue her. I will never forget praying (and journaling), "Lord, give Minnie what she needs, no matter what that looks like." When I prayed that prayer, I had a foreboding feeling that someone I loved would have to endure suffering or even die so that she would finally come to the end of herself. I begged and pleaded with God that it would be me who suffered or died, and not my husband or one of our other children. I would never have imagined it would be Minnie because of how I perceived God's promise of Psalm 27:13. I would have gladly given my life to see Minnie live. Funny how God rarely answers our prayers the way we think He will or should. But that is the thing about trust. Do we believe God is who He says He is and that His promises are faithful and true? He promised I would see His goodness in the land of the living. It admittedly had a different meaning than I imagined . . . but I truly have seen His goodness, even though the heart-wrenching pain.

4

MY PRAYER JOURNAL

I am so grateful I put my prayers on paper so I could go back and see where my heart was every day and how God answered prayer, often *not* how I expected. Join me on this journey through my unbelievable agony and grief as I worked out my own faith and, like Jacob, wrestled with God over the years in the darkest valley.

As everything with Minnie started speeding up, I recorded every deep and painful prayer I cried to the Lord. You will see that my faith was tested over and over (and sadly, I often gave in to fear until the Lord took hold of my anxious heart). I hope this helps you see you are not alone in what you may be experiencing as you read this. I pray some of the ways the Lord spoke to me will also help you in your times of confusion, anger, questioning, and fear. As hard as this was to revisit and record for you, it also gave me so much hope, seeing how God

> *"What has happened to me has really served to advance the gospel."*

truly did answer my prayers and kept His promises. I know He will continue to do so as I navigate the future of a life without my Minnie—but knowing ultimately it will be a future *with* her!

I have also added some of the excerpts from the devotionals I was reading throughout the year so you can see how God used them to speak directly to me.

JUNE 1, 2022

Many of my friends are lost without You and don't even know it. Lord, I pray for the boldness of Your Holy Spirit to say what they need to hear. Let Your Spirit speak through me! Let me see the souls saved of those I love so dearly.

[I had no idea the boldness would come through the loss of my Minnie. Immediately after her death I held nothing back; the words just flowed, and I knew my friends could see my genuine heart of love for them. I am still praying for all of them and I know I will see salvation come!]

JULY 29, 2022

Lord, I don't need to keep stating my requests in detail. You know what they are and You know my heart. Currently one of my favorite songs is "Jireh" (Elevation Worship, Maverick City Music 2021) because You are telling me that in every circumstance You are enough. I pray my will would align with Yours because You and only You know how to work out everything for my good and Your glory. I realize I have no control over how or when You will do it; all I know is that You will do it and Your timing will be perfect. And when You do finally do it and I see my prayers answered, I will be in awe of how You worked it out so perfectly, as I've seen You do many times in the past. When circumstances seem darkest with no answers, that is when You show Yourself most glorious and powerful. I'm longing for that day.

[August 10, 2022, was the day before Minnie's birthday and the day her best friend and sister moved to Texas. She lost "her person" that day, and between Francesca leaving and the new boy who would soon come into her life, she started the freefall into her destructive behavior that would eventually steal her from me.]

Minnie wrote a poem for her sister just before she left. You can feel her heartbreak in her beautiful words.

THE EMPTY ROOM

I walk into your room and smell the flowers that were once there
But nothing is stronger than the memories we used to share
I could let go and leave you in my past
But the smell of the flowers brings me right back
I remember your smile and the sound of your laughter
The way your blue eyes melted into green
And yellow after
I could forget you and the time we spent together
But that won't do me any better
The cold breeze comes through your window
And I look out and see your shadow
The wind blows through your hair

AUGUST 21, 2022

God, once again I lift my Minnie to You. . . . I know the answer [to her problems] yet I can't tell her anything else because it makes her mad and pushes her away. O God, she needs You! Help her to see it! Bring her to the end of herself. God, save my baby's soul. Save her to the uttermost, as only You can. Heal all her wounds. Give her a new life. Give her freedom from her bondage. Even when I don't see it, You're working.

[This was my prayer the day after she told me about the new boy she was talking to. She told me while we were with her therapist because she knew I would not be happy. He was at the continuation high school, "clean" after being a drug user, with a schizophrenic mother, addict father, being raised by his grandmother who had now passed away, and at the time living with his alcoholic uncle who really wanted nothing to do with him. What was there to be concerned about? As time went on I learned that this was just the tip of the iceberg, that he was a heavy drug user and dealer, a thief, verbally and physically abusive, and certainly a significant reason my Minnie is no longer here.]

AUGUST 30, 2022

Lord, today I listened to a [pastor].... He was talking about his son who is not a believer and said God woke him up one night and spoke to him as clear as day: "He's not yours—he's Mine. So be still." O God, I believe this for Minnie! I've done all I can humanly do, but now I have to just let You deal with her as only a perfect and loving heavenly Father can do, and You know best—You know exactly what she needs to come home. I open my hands and release her back to You. Lord, care for her and protect her. I know it's her soul both You and I are most concerned about, but I pray You would keep her safe while she wanders. I will be still.

[I did not know that God would have to take her to save her. When I prayed, it was her soul that both God and I were most concerned about. But through so many horrible situations, He really did keep her safe and brought her, finally, to that perfect moment in time He had determined her rescue.]

SEPTEMBER 9, 2022

Lord, Minnie is super-low again, and I am desperate for You to move. You keep telling me to wait on You, and I am waiting, expecting, knowing the victory is coming—but I am desperate! You're all I have, yet You are all I need. There is nothing in this world that will ever satisfy her, help her, make her happy, or make her whole—nothing but You alone! Make her realize that aside from You there is no help in her therapy, in her medication, in her friends, or in her boyfriend. Draw her to You as only You can. She is so lost but You know where she is and how to bring her home. I will never stop praying and never stop hoping. "Donna, against all hope, in hope believed."

SEPTEMBER 30, 2022

Lord, she is spiraling out of control. Darkness surrounds her and I can see the torment—*but God!* I have faith in Your promises because You've never failed and You won't start now. My eyes lie to me when I see her life and the hopelessness in her because my mind remembers what You've done and hope tells me You'll do it again—and hope does not disappoint!

NOVEMBER 4, 2022

Of all the times I was at my end before, this one is right there with the worst of them. O Lord, save my Minnie! I can't even put it into words, but You see and know. You said the Holy Spirit intercedes for me with groans even when I don't have the words. I have nothing left.

[I don't even recall the situation at this time since there were so many highs and lows. My memory is lost in all the storms. If only I knew that a year later my "nothing left" would be at a whole new level. He emptied me more and more throughout the entire year.]

NOVEMBER 11, 2022

Wow! I missed reading yesterday so I needed to go back and read November 10 today in my devotional. Before I opened it, I prayed, "Lord, make my heart steadfast and not let my hope fail for Minnie." After I prayed I opened the book to November 10—"Against all hope, Abraham in hope believed" (Romans 4:18 NIV)—the verse that kept me going in the past and let me know I don't hope in what I see. Even when it appears it is all falling apart, I still hope in You and Your promises. Lord, You speak so loudly to me, and I am so thankful!

NOVEMBER 22, 2023

Well, God, You did it again! I'm sitting here looking over Facebook memories, but not until I read my devotional. You gave me the verse Matthew 9:28: "Do you believe I am able to do this?" and also Jeremiah 32:27: "Is anything too hard for Me?" Then I went to my Facebook memories and there it was, my post nine years ago during another dark and desperate time in my life: "Is anything too hard for Me?" Lord, You continue to speak to me loud and clear and You continue to amaze me. I know You are working and I long for that day I see my Minnie saved. It's coming! Amen!

NOVEMBER 27, 2022

Lord, does it have to get worse before it gets better? Minnie just had a major meltdown where she said she wanted to die. She was screaming and shaking. I didn't know what to do, so I went and put my hands on her and prayed for Your peace to fill her mind and heart. I bound darkness in Jesus's name, and I prayed she would feel Your love. She sat there and let me pray and she seemed to calm down. I just reminded her how much I love her and need her. Lord, I pray she would call out to You even now. Bind the darkness in her life. Strip her of everything that takes her from You, and bring my girl back to You and back to me. Preserve her life as You work on her heart and mind.

[I believe You certainly did preserve her life for another year, during which time I know You spoke to her and revealed Yourself to her over and over again. That is why she told one of her best friends shortly before her passing that she wanted to go back to church. She had even told me about a month before she left this earth that she was thinking about getting baptized.]

DECEMBER 4, 2022

Lord, having finished reading through the Bible, I decided to write down all the names You revealed and the names others called You in the Scriptures. I was thinking about what that all means and who You are to me. You are everything I need in every season of my life, but right now here are Your names I need to know most of all: Savior, Provider, Healer, Bondage-Breaker, Strength and Shield, Peace, My Place of Safety, The God Who Sees Me, Faithful God, My Helper, The God Who Shows Me Unfailing Love, Merciful, The God Who Saves, The Lamb Who Takes Away the Sins of the World, Advocate, High Priest, The God Who Pays Back Those Who Harm Me, The God Who Declares Me Innocent, Gracious and Merciful God, My Song, Redeemer, The One Who Comforts, Word of Life, Love. There are so many more, but these speak most loudly to me right now, but the awesome thing is that wherever I am in my life, whatever I need, that is who You are to me. You truly are all I need, and because You are faithful, I know I can trust You are who You say You are!

[There was a brief period here when Minnie broke up with *him* for the first time of many. With her mind now clear, she told me what a horrible and evil person he really was. She never told me what he had done but she said over and over what a horrible person he was. Toward her he was controlling, mean, and aggressive, and that is why she left him—but that demonic stronghold pulled her back and led to the next dreadful events.]

DECEMBER 30, 2022

Lord, in the history of the worst weeks in my life, this is in the top two. I went from such a high on Christmas to one of my lowest lows the next several days—eighteen hours in the emergency room sitting by her side, praying and crying over her as she slept; praying deliverance over the demonic bondage in her life and sure that she would wake up ready to run to Jesus. We had some good talks when she woke up, and she wanted to join the family at the cabin. We had such a wonderful drive together, talking all the way up the mountain, and I felt she might be coming around.

Then she said she was spending the night at her friend's house again last night, and sure enough, she went to see *him* instead. We texted her friend, who confirmed she was not there, and she found Minnie's phone in the bushes where she had tossed it. Steve and I immediately got in the car to go rescue her from his hold, knowing it could mean a violent confrontation. I called our therapist, and she talked me down because she kept saying, "He's not worth going to jail over. You won't be any good to Minnie if you're in jail." We finally picked her up the next day in an Albertson's parking lot and drove straight to the therapist. She kept asking Minnie what she was using because she saw in her eyes it was more than marijuana. Minnie never admitted to anything more.

And here I am in my brokenness reaching out to You not only for her but also for me. The verse of the day on KLOVE radio today was Psalm 34:6 (NLT): "In my desperation I prayed, and the Lord listened; He saved me from all my troubles." I read the whole chapter, and verses 18 and 19 say, "The Lord is close to the brokenhearted; He rescues those whose spirits are crushed. The righteous person faces many troubles but the Lord comes to the rescue each time." Lord, I'm desperate!

[I remember vividly the events of the week. Since she had been dating the new boyfriend, the physical changes in her were drastic. Her once-beautiful skin turned thick and pitted, and she lost a significant amount of weight. We would learn this was from not only heavy drug use but also the anorexia and bulimia that had taken hold of her. We still enjoyed a beautiful Christmas, but she kept asking all day when we would be leaving because she wanted to spend the night at her friend's house. Later that evening we dropped her off at her friend's, but both Steve and I had our suspicions. We picked her up the day after Christmas, and we were getting ready to head up to the family cabin . . . until Minnie cried out for me from the bathroom! I ran in to see the deepest cut, gushing blood, on her forearm. I immediately applied pressure and yelled for Steve to call 911. They sent paramedics and police, and as soon as the police saw her arm, they placed her on a 5150 hold and rushed her to the hospital for stitches. This is an involuntary seventy-two-hour hospitalization for someone experiencing a mental health crisis. I sat with her all night praying over her while she slept. The following day the hospital psychologist came, and after speaking with her, he released her because he determined she was not trying to take her life. At the time of her hospitalization she tested positive only for marijuana. However, looking back now, I believe what her therapist saw in her eyes was heavy amounts of Percocet combined with who-knows-what-else-he-had-given-her.

From this point on the downhill spiral became furious, and I was just trying to keep her alive and keep my head barely above water each day.]

JANUARY 1, 2023

"The land you are . . . to take possession of is a land of mountains and valleys that drinks rain from heaven. It is a land the Lord your God cares for; the eyes of the Lord your God are continually on it from the beginning of the year to its end" (Deuteronomy 11:11–12 NIV). Today we stand at the threshold of the unknown. Before us lies a new year, and we are going forward to take possession of it. Who knows what we will find? . . . The Lord is to be our Source of supply. . . . The land we are to possess is a land of valleys and hills. . . . We need [both] the valleys and hills. . . . We cannot see what loss, sorrow, and trials are accomplishing. We need only to trust (Cowman 13).

[I could never have imagined what the coming year would bring, but I am so thankful the Lord gave me this devotion at the beginning to remind me that in everything that would happen—and will happen—He is accomplishing something greater than we could ever imagine and "the eyes of the Lord your God are continually on it from the beginning of the year to its end."]

JANUARY 3, 2023

"I [will] move along slowly at the pace…of the children" (Genesis 33:14 NIV). We have never been this way before, but the Lord Jesus has. . . . He knows the steep places that take our breath away, the rocky paths that make our feet ache, the hot and shadeless stretches that bring us to exhaustion, and the rushing rivers that we have to cross—Jesus has gone through it all before us . . . and will never make you take even one step beyond what your feet are able to endure. Never mind if you think you are unable to take another step, for either He will strengthen you to make you able, or He will call a sudden halt, and you will not have to take it at all (Cowman 16).

JANUARY 4, 2023

"Jesus replied, 'You may go. Your son will live.' The man took Jesus at His word and departed" (John 4:50 NIV). "Whatever you ask for in prayer, believe" (Mark 11:24 NIV). When you are confronted with a matter that requires immediate prayer, pray until you believe God—until with wholehearted sincerity you can thank Him for the answer. . . . There is nothing that so fully solidifies faith as being so sure of the answer that you can thank God for it. . . . The type of prayer that empties us of faith frequently arises from focusing our thoughts on the difficulty rather than on God's promise (Cowman 17).

See Romans 4:19–20 NIV regarding Abraham: "He did not waver through unbelief regarding the promise of God." *Faith is not a sense, nor sight, nor reason, but simply taking God at His word* (quoted in Cowman 18). *The beginning of anxiety is the end of faith, and the beginning of true faith is the end of anxiety* (quoted in Cowman 18). . . . *You will never learn faith in comfortable surroundings.*

It's hard to even put into words what has happened. On January 2 Minnie was acting strange, and I knew something was wrong. After a series of things we discovered early yesterday morning, she ran away and we tried everything to find her. In our hearts we knew she was with *him*. She texted to tell us she was okay, but that was all the information she gave us. Lord, only You know what we went through—all the pain, heartache, and emotions. Finally, my sister's husband called her, and she actually took his call, listened to him, and poured out her heart. He was able to speak some tough love to her, as well as give Steve and me more insight into her and how her mind operated. However, she was still not speaking to us, nor was she coming home. Finally, this morning, the boyfriend's uncle came to the door to tell us she had been living there, but he was afraid of trouble since she was only seventeen, so he kicked them both out. She ran away from her home with a family who adored her but then got kicked out of her runaway home. This evening the uncle brought her home. Minnie, Steve, and I sat for hours and had one of the best talks we've ever had. We reminded her of how much we believe in her and that her past does not define her. We encouraged her and loved on her. Trust will have to be earned. Jesus, do the work! I praise You in advance for the miracle You're going to do and have already started to do. This is the turning point—I believe it!

[Like all the other turning points and rock bottoms, she soon settled back into her lies and self-deception. It seemed that each time she slid backward it was farther back than she had been before.]

JANUARY 6, 2023

Lord, as I wait on You I find You are doing a work in me. As I was driving today I came to the realization that there is nothing I can do—but then Your peace washed over me as I realized that I'm so glad it's not in my hands, because I don't know which way to turn. But You told me to give You my burdens and leave them at Your feet, so that's what I did. Knowing that I don't have to deal with it anymore is an amazing feeling. You are not worried because You know just what to do, and in fact You're already doing it. So now I sit back and pray (which is my part) and I watch You work in the most miraculous way, things I never could have accomplished or even thought of on my own. Isaiah 43:19 says, "I am about to do something new. See, I have already begun! Do you not see it? I will make a pathway through the wilderness. I will create rivers in the dry wasteland" (NLT).

[Nothing from this point to the point of Minnie's passing seemed as if God was working. The lows to follow were lower than anything I had ever experienced. I don't know what I ever would have done without the reassurance that God is faithful and is always working on my behalf, even when I cannot see Him moving. Isaiah 43:2 says, "When you pass through the waters . . . they will not sweep over you" (NIV). This isn't "if" but "when." The priests had to step into the Jordan before God stopped up the waters so they could cross. I had to be in the floodwaters to see the miracles of God.]

JANUARY 13, 2023

"In all these things we are more than conquerors through him who loved us" (Romans 8:37 NIV). This is more than victory. This is a triumph so complete that we not only have escaped defeat and destruction but also have destroyed our enemies and won plunder so rich and valuable that we can actually thank God for the battle. . . . "What has happened to me has really served to advance the gospel" (Philippians 1:12 NIV). (Cowman 29, 30).

[I later made a note here in 2024 that I am waiting for the salvation of so many as the plunder from the enemy! In the end what matters most is that my Minnie is with Jesus, and because of her and our story, there will be many who find Him.]

JANUARY 14, 2023

"The . . . shepherd always walked ahead of his sheep. He was always out in front. Any attack upon the sheep had to take him into account first. Now God is out in front. He is in our tomorrows, and it is tomorrow that fills people with fear. Yet God is already there. All the tomorrows of our life have to pass through Him before they can get to us" (quoted in Cowman 32).

[Reading this again in 2024, I noted, "Oh, if only I had quoted this every single day of this year, I would not have been tossed back and forth by the storms that hit each day. The Lord was in every moment, in every 'tomorrow'; He was walking out in front so that no attack came to me without first going through Him.]

JANUARY 15, 2023

Lord, today You have spoken to me in several ways! First, You gave me Psalm 143:8—"Let the morning bring me word of your unfailing love, for I have put my trust in you. Show me the way I should go, for to you I entrust my life" (NIV). Then in church we sang "I Ran Out of That Grave" (Passion, Stanfill 2017) and I pictured You calling Minnie's name and her running to You—then immediately Mom texted me (she was watching online) and said, "Minnie will run out of the darkness into His glorious day." What a confirmation! Then when pastor spoke, he talked about how for some of us our mission field is in our own home with an unsaved loved one. He said to never give up on them.

[Little did I know that in ten short months God would call her name and she would run out of that grave! Let this also be a word to you, parents, that not all of us have a mission field to the far corners of the world. For some of us our most important ministry is right there in our own homes. Don't lose sight of that calling because you feel that God isn't using you out in the world. As a mom I have one main purpose in life, and that is to do all I can to make sure my children spend eternity in heaven.]

JANUARY 27, 2023

Lord, my prayer is simple, but I'm also asking big because You are a great God, who raised Jesus from the grave! Remove this boy from Minnie's life immediately—far, far away, where he can't hurt her anymore—then do the mighty miraculous work of saving her and healing her scars (mental, spiritual, and physical). To me it seems impossible, but with You nothing is impossible!

I need You to be the same God You were to Jacob, Joshua, Daniel, David, and so many others. You did big miracles for them, but for Minnie, she needs You to show up as You did for the woman at the well (John 4). I know You will meet her where she is and speak to all her pain. I believe it!

FEBRUARY 1, 2023

Lord, You blessed me in a big way this week! Minnie stayed home from school Monday because she was physically and emotionally spent from binging and purging all night. But she sat out with me while I worked all day and we had the best and longest conversation we've ever had. The best part is that we talked about You! I told her to pray that You would make Yourself real to her, that You would reveal who You are—and Lord, I pray that over her, even if she doesn't pray it for herself. Break through the darkness and hardness of heart, break through her own thoughts and ideas and give her a new heart and a new mind. I know You are working in her life. Do great things with her for Your kingdom.

[My prayer wasn't answered the way I thought it would be, but I do certainly see that God is using her life, and particularly her death, to move upon the hearts of those around me.]

FEBRUARY 6, 8, 2023

How close God is to us through His promises, and how brightly those promises shine! Yet during times of prosperity, we lose sight of their brilliance. In the way the sun at noon hides the stars from sight, His promises become indiscernible. But when night falls—the deep, dark night of sorrow—a host of stars begin to shine, bringing forth God's blessed constellations of hope, and promises of comfort from His Word.

[This would become more and more true as this year would go on, and all I would have to grasp onto for dear life was—and still is—His amazing and sustaining promises.]

Do not look ahead to what may happen tomorrow. The same everlasting Father who cares for you today will take care of you tomorrow. . . . Either He will shield you from suffering or He will give you His unwavering strength that you may bear it (Cowman 63, 65).

[Over the course of several years, and 2023 in particular, He certainly did not shield me from one ounce of suffering, but somehow, as you will understand as you continue to read, His strength was made perfect in all my weakness. There is nothing within me that could withstand all I went through—only Christ in me!]

FEBRUARY 9, 2023

Lord, my relationship with Minnie has grown! We've spent so much time together and we've talked so much. Some huge things have happened! The other day she was sitting out in the kitchen with me and she said, "Home used to be the last place I wanted to be. Now I just want to be here sitting and talking to you all day." My heart nearly exploded!

[Obviously this was a moment of lucidity for her, because when she was using whatever drug she was on, I can tell you that home was the *last* place she wanted to be.]

Then a Facebook memory popped up from ten years ago in which I stated, "Patience is doing what I can do while I wait for

God to do what only He can do." Yes! And then three more times this same day You gave me the word that You are doing this in Your perfect timing and I need to wait on You. Then the best thing—she broke up with him again! She is sad but she knows this is good. I pray You fill her lonely heart as only You can do. God is on the move!

[Friend, I hope you can see how God was preparing my heart for what was to come. I'm so thankful I put all of this down on paper because during times of desperation, I could barely breathe, let alone remember these little daily miracles.]

FEBRUARY 14, 2023

Here I am again, Lord, with my head in my hands and my heart broken. I got a call from school to pick up Minnie because she was caught at school with weed, vape, and cigarettes—suspended with a court date and community service. I picked her up and told her if she doesn't throw all of it away, there is no car and no New York trip, (I had booked a graduation trip for her and me, and we were so excited to spend that time together soon!) I am at my end. The coddling time is over and it's time for tough love. Lord, I need help, wisdom, guidance, answers, peace, strength. Just when I thought we had some positive movement, this was a huge slap in the face. I don't know how much more hurt I can take. I'm empty, just a shell of myself. How many times will You allow me to be crushed? Yet "though he slay me, yet will I hope in him" (Job 13:15 NIV).

[This was the yo-yo of my life the last couple years. However, you can see that my problem was I allowed my emotional state to be dictated by her actions, and it nearly killed me. Please learn this lesson from me. Allow God to steady your soul so you aren't tossed back and forth the way I was too many times.]

FEBRUARY 16, 2023

Lord, as You always do, You take something horrible and turn it for good. Minnie and I ended up having a wonderful text conversation last night, and I really feel she is moving in the right direction. She even told me she enjoyed watching church online with me last week and that if I stay home again this week, she will watch with me. I love being in church, but if she is willing to do this with me, then I have to be there for her. Lord, keep working on her heart because nothing else matters. I am rejoicing in advance; a sacrifice of thanksgiving for her complete healing!

FEBRUARY 21, 2023

Lord, I've never seen anything like this. The binging and purging has gotten so bad she quit her job because she cannot function. I'm over here trying to just keep her alive, but I remind myself a thousand times a day that it's nothing I can do but something only You can handle—so I'm begging You to do it, Lord! I'm sinking so fast; I can't keep my head above water. Lord, deliver her please! My beautiful baby—she just lies in bed in a pile of filth and doesn't even care. Rescue her from the pit, my Savior! And rescue me.

[Looking back at all my prayers begging God to rescue her, I realize now that He did it the best way possible. There is no greater rescue than taking a broken soul out of this world and bringing her into new life.]

MARCH 4, 2023

Lord, tonight Minnie lied and snuck out with *him* again, and we basically hunted them down and drove her home. We gave her a choice—him or us. They used drugs again, so I called him and said that if he ever contacts her in any way again, I will have him arrested for giving drugs to a minor. I lost any cool I had left and really let him have it! She heard me make the call and I told her that if she chooses him, she becomes a renter in our home and pays for everything, or she completely cuts it off with him and we pick up the pieces of our shattered relationship once again. After some time, she came into our room and said, "I choose you."

[She did cut it off with him for quite some time, only to make other horrible mistakes. I feel like her self-worth was completely destroyed and she was unable to make good choices in guys. She did not know what it was like to be treated properly, so she fell for anyone who gave her attention.]

MARCH 8, 2023

Every promise of God's is built on four pillars. The first two are His justice and holiness, which will never allow Him to deceive us. The third is His grace or goodness, which will not allow Him to forget. And the fourth is His truth, which will not allow Him to change (quoted in Cowman 104).

[As I have said so many times, God's promises are like a check that just needs to be brought to the bank to be cashed. When God made such great promises in His Word, and then He impressed certain ones on my heart, I can be confident that He will do as He said! That is why we are to walk by faith. We get into trouble when we allow our feelings to dictate our walk, as you will see in my own life throughout this year of great trials and testing. Our feelings will try to dissuade us from the *fact* of God's presence. That's why we have to anchor to the Rock, especially in times of trouble. Matthew Henry said, "When I cannot feel the faith of assurance, I live by the fact of God's faithfulness" (quoted in Cowman 108).]

MARCH 18, 2023

Lord, knowing You've already won this battle is the only thing that keeps me going. You've promised, You've shown Your wonders in the past, so I believe it! Yesterday "the boy" sent her texts threatening her and me, and we had to call the police and make a report. I think the fact that he threatened me really shook her, and she realized the trouble she has brought on all of us by her decisions. I think that was the breaking point, and I'm thankful You caused it to be dramatic and final—that's exactly what she needed, and now I see she has moved on and her load is lighter.

[Unfortunately, the stronghold he had on her kept her going back to him over and over again, no matter what he said or did to her. The moment he came into her life in August 2022 is when everything got dark, toxic, and destructive.]

However, she is still dealing with the eating disorder in ways none of us can imagine. I pray in the name of Jesus for her complete deliverance from that addiction. I look forward to that day when she rededicates her life to Jesus, gets baptized, and I see her free from her bondage.

MARCH 21, 2023

Lord, I need You to rescue Minnie! Her bulimia is out of control—she has been on a horrible downward spiral for several days and can't stop on her own. God, she needs You but won't call out. Please intrude into her world before she destroys herself. God, I'm calling out for her, I'm pleading on behalf of her—Lord, show up huge for her, and let her see You and run to You. There is no other way out for her. Let her see her desperation and come to You. I'm desperate for You, Lord; I'm desperate.

[Although it was eight months later, and I cannot be sure, I truly feel this is what happened that night You took her home. She cried out in desperation and You came to her rescue.]

MARCH 28, 2023

Here I am again, Lord, and I feel like a whining kid, begging for something from her parent. God, I need Your help—so desperately! I need Your wisdom of how to deal with Minnie. I've been scared, angry, concerned, loving, coddling—but none of it is working.

I want to come down hard on her, but then I want to open my arms and hold her. I want to push her away and tell her to get out, but then I want to hold on tightly and never let go. God, I'm hurting—I'm desperate, I'm lost, I want to give up, but I can't. Day and night I'm filled with a heaviness that is weighing me down to the point that I'm always sick. I can't do this anymore; it's too much for me to bear.

MARCH 29, 2023

Lord, send Minnie what she needs! Far be it for me to tell You what she needs and how to help her. You made her and You know just what she needs. Lord, send Minnie what she needs!

[This was the hardest prayer I ever prayed for her, and I had no idea what it would eventually mean. However, I had a feeling that by releasing her to God this way would mean some dreaded grief—I just didn't know what. After I prayed this prayer I read the following words in my devotional:

> When we are in darkness, the temptation is to find our own way without trusting in the Lord and relying upon Him. Instead of allowing Him to help us, we try to help ourselves. We seek the light of the natural way and the advice of our friends. We reason out our own conclusions and thereby may be tempted to accept a path of deliverance that would not be of God at all. . . . Beloved, never try to get out of a dark place except in God's timing and in His way. (Cowman 134)

Wow! God surely spoke deeply to me in many ways about hindering His work by trying to help Him.]

APRIL 12, 2023

Lord, I haven't had much to write in regard to Minnie because it's just been so bad—weeks of binging and purging and now several days without eating. She's been mean and defensive, and she didn't even get out of bed to be with her sister before she left for school again. I've realized, however, that nothing I do or say helps in any way, and so my prayer day and night has just been "Lord, send Minnie what she needs!" I give it all up—it's on You, God. But I'm holding You to Your promise that I will see her salvation before I die. I'm sure You spoke to me and gave me that promise, so I take that check to the bank to cash it in!

[When I started praying that prayer, my faith got strengthened and more resolute. It was at this point I stopped trying to direct God and started just hanging on tightly to His promises.]

APRIL 16, 2023

Lord, I'm weary! I feel as though You've given me a promise that I would see Minnie's coming back to You and her healing, but was that actually a word from You?—because all I see is her getting worse. I don't want to give myself false hope—did You really give me that promise or was that my own voice talking to myself? Lord, Gideon asked twice for a sign to know if it was really You speaking, so like him, I'm asking. Please give me a sign so I can know it is really Your voice, Your promise for me. I need to hear from You loud and clear, Lord.

[Then after I wrote this prayer, I read my devotional for two days, April 15 and 16, because I had missed a day of reading.

> April 15: Psalm 119:42—*I trust in Your word.* The strength of our faith is in direct proportion to our level of belief that God will do exactly what He has promised. Faith has nothing to do with feelings,

impressions, outward appearances, nor the probability or improbability of an event. If we try to couple these things with faith, we are no longer resting on the Word of God, because faith is not dependent on them. Faith rests on the pure Word of God alone. And when we take Him at His Word, our hearts are at peace. (Cowman 156)

April 16: Hebrews 11:8 (NIV)—*By faith Abraham, when called to go to a place he would later receive as his inheritance, obeyed and went, even though he did not know where he was going.* Abraham . . . did not lean as much on the promises as he did on the Promiser. And he did not look at the difficulties of his circumstances but looked to His King—the eternal, limitless, invisible, wise, and only God—who had reached down from His throne to direct his path and who would certainly prove Himself. . . . You must also be willing to take your ideas of what the journey will be like and tear them into tiny pieces, for nothing on the itinerary will happen as you expect. Your Guide will not keep to any beaten path. He will lead you through ways you would never have dreamed your eyes would see. He knows no fear, and He expects you to fear nothing while He is with you. (Cowman 157, 158)]

APRIL 18, 2023

Lord, as I've been searching for help and begging You to show me Your promises, You gave me two things as I lay bed unable to sleep. First, I know Minnie gave her heart to You as a child! You told me last night in Philippians 1:6, "being confident of this, that He who began a good work in you will complete it" (Psalm 27:13–14, paraphrased). Lord, You began the good work in her years ago, so I will trust this promise that You will be faithful to complete it! Also, the words to the song "Promise Keeper" (Darst 2020) ran over and over in my head.

[This song has been on repeat in my head and heart ever since that night. Worship music is vital to our weary souls! Especially the ones with scripture imbedded in them like this one. The words will come back just when you need them and lift up your heart. Never neglect worship!]

APRIL 19, 2022

"Thus says the Lord God, 'Indeed I Myself will search for My sheep and seek them out'" (Ezekiel 34:11). Jesus is great as a seeking Shepherd as well as a saving Shepherd. Though many of those His Father gave Him have gone as near to hell's gate as they possibly can, yet the Lord by searching and seeking finds them and draws near to them in grace. He has sought us out. Let us have good hope for those who are pressed upon our hearts in prayer, for He will find them also. . . . He will by providence and grace pursue them into foreign lands, into places of poverty, into dens of obscurity, and into depths of despair. He will not lose one of all whom the Father has given Him (Spurgeon 117). (Then I wrote in the margin, "Lord, seek Minnie! Amen!")

[Wow! Looking back at this gave me chills. This was basically Minnie's story, and as promised, Jesus did not lose her but sought her out from the depths of her despair.]

APRIL 27, 2023

Lord, it's a daily struggle trying to fight myself to stop trying to take this weight back on myself. I've given it to You so many times and I know You are the promise keeper—I know You work all things for good because I love You. I know that You're not pacing around heaven worrying about what to do next because You already know the ending, and You are just moving the chess pieces into place. I know You love her more than I ever could. I know You are good, faithful merciful, and love. I know You see my hurt, but You have promised to give me help, hope, strength, and a future. I know You've promised to restore what the locust have destroyed (Joel 2:25–27). I know I will see the goodness of the Lord in the land of the living (Psalm 27:13).

[I would never have made it through these battles, and certainly not the biggest trial of losing Minnie, without being rooted in scripture every single day! All of these things I prayed were just stating scripture back to God, reminding Him of His promises, something He *wants* us to do!]

APRIL 30, 2023

Lord, You sent Minnie what she needed—a severe bleeding ulcer. She was up all night throwing up blood, and now she is in the most severe pain, but she is aware she caused it and is ready to turn it around. Once again, You did what I could never do. All it took was me laying her at Your feet and surrendering to You. You know exactly what You are doing and I can confidently leave her in Your hands.

[Both Minnie and I realized after this latest hospitalization that we needed to cancel our long-awaited New York trip. She knew her health was failing, and we both knew there was not much lower she could go. I encouraged her that this was just a *postponed* trip and that we would eventually go celebrate her. She would end up missing every major milestone this year, and I told her that as soon as she got completely better we would have the biggest and best celebration ever for her. What I didn't realize until later was that the celebration would be four hundred people attending her celebration of life when the Lord completely healed her once and for all.]

MAY 2, 2023

God . . . walking into my child's room and seeing her eyes rolled back in her head, mouth gaping open, unresponsive, and totally limp—I shouted at her, slapped her face, dumped cold water on her. We called 911 and they all showed up with the police. Minnie revived and then was irrationally furious, saying (shouting) the most horrible things ever to me. "We do not know what to do, but our eyes are upon You. . . . The battle is not yours but God's. . . . Position yourselves, stand still and see the salvation of the Lord, who is with you" (2 Chronicles 20:12, 15, 17). "In returning and rest you shall be saved, in quietness and trust shall be your strength" (Isaiah 30:15). My hope is only in Christ! And then the Lord led me to this quote from Charles H. Spurgeon: "My situation is urgent, and I cannot see how I will ever be delivered. Yet this is not my concern, for He who made the promise will find a way to keep it. My part is simply to obey His commands, not to direct His ways. I am His servant, not His advisor. I call upon Him and He will deliver me" (quoted in Cowman 180).

[Up until the day I found her gone, this was the scariest, most horrific moment of my life. Maybe, most likely, God was preparing me for what was to come. But what He tenderly spoke to me is that He will keep His promises, no matter how dire the situation is. It is this hope that kept me going every day, not knowing what the next day would bring—but I knew, and still know and believe, that anything that comes my way is "Jesus-filtered." In other words, if something comes to me, it has to go through Him first.]

MAY 9, 2023

Sometimes I wonder if You hear me, Lord. The harder I pray and come against the enemy, the worse it gets. I know You are God, You are good, You are love, and You are faithful—but I just don't understand. Her problems are ripping me apart. Her rebellion is my sleepless nights. Her rejection of You is my greatest heartache. Her lies are the gaping wounds to my soul. Her self-destruction is my deepest pain. I need You to move in her heart. . . . I'm holding You to Your promises. I have no other hope.

MAY 10, 2023

Lord, You know this has been the most discouraging week, and I am asking You again if You hear me when I cry out to You. God, please hear me; answer my prayer. I need You! After I wrote this prayer, as usual I opened my devotional book and this was the reading for that day: "I would have lost heart unless I had believed that I would see the goodness of the Lord in the land of the living. Wait on the Lord; be of good courage, and He shall strengthen your heart" (Psalm 27:13–14). [There it was! *My promise!* God spoke it back to me at the moment I needed it so much! The devotional went on to say, "Once you have come close to the point of despair, God's message is not, 'Be strong and courageous' (Joshua 1:6), for He knows that your strength and courage have run away. Instead, He says sweetly, 'Be still, and know that I am God' (Psalm 46:10)" (Cowman 188).]

MAY 11, 2023

"We don't know what to do but our eyes are on you" (2 Chronicles 20:12 NIV). [See how many times I quoted this scripture. Again, we need God's Word deep in our hearts because it will be there when we need it!] Lord, Your Word is a lamp to my feet, lighting up my next step and not the entire trail. So much has happened the last couple days, and I am feeling a strong pull toward getting her into a residential facility. My heart and my mind are struggling with all the details—school, vacation, work, doing it before she turns 18—but I feel that it is the most loving thing I can do to get her the help she doesn't want. Lord, if this is Your will (and I do *not* want to do it if it isn't), please let all the pieces fall into place. Her caring boss already said there will be a place for her at work when she gets back. Now I am asking You to work out all the rest of the details. Not my will but Yours be done.

MAY 12, 2023

Lord, my eyes tell me that Minnie is lost, broken beyond all repair, destroyed, sinking ever deeper every day. Everything she does is leading her deeper into the pit, and I know she feels the despair—but it is always darkest before the dawn! I know hope is on the horizon—I can feel it rising in my soul, even as the circumstances get more desperate. Now all I need is for You to fit all the pieces into place for me so my steps are crystal clear. Open doors and shut others so I will be 100-percent confident that I am in Your will. If You're not in it, then I don't want to go—I cannot go! Give me wisdom and discernment more than ever before, Lord. I'm counting on You with all I am.

MAY 16, 2023

> Daniel 10:12 (NIV)—*Do not be afraid, Daniel. Since the first day that you set your mind to . . . humble yourself before your God, your words were heard, and I have come in response to them.* "Many prayers of believers are hindered by Satan. Yet you do not need to fear when your unanswered prayers are piling up, for soon they will break through like a flood. When that happens, not only will your answers flow through but they will also be accompanied by new blessings." (quoted in Cowman 197)

[I had no idea at the time how true this would be. I had been fasting and praying every week without fail since 2021, waiting for the answers, that huge breakthrough. I never stopped until the day all the answers came through like a flood the day Jesus took Minnie home. Fasting aligned my will with God's and allowed Him to work the outcome His way, the best possible way. And then He gave me these verses, again, while I did not know how profound this would become to me in the near future: *We were under great pressure . . . so that we despaired even of life. . . . But this happened that we might not rely on ourselves but on God, who raises the dead* (2 Corinthians 1:8–9 NIV).]

MAY 17, 2023

Lord, remind me You're here! Minnie is spiraling out of control and my emotions are all over the place. I got a call today that Minnie might not graduate because she isn't meeting with teachers or turning in work. [At this point she was on medical home study.] Every single day I wake up wondering what's next—how low can You possibly take me before I break? You promised to give me strength for anything, but I'm not handling this! I'm ready to break! How much more, Lord? How much more?

MAY 24, 2023

Our anniversary and Minnie's graduation day. It seems like a perfect day to celebrate—in a world that's not turned upside down! I'm sitting here crying out to You, Lord. I'm literally weeping when I should be going to graduation—*if* Minnie were actually going! Just another crack in this glass of my life that is already shattering. How is it that You can allow so much pain before You move? How many rock bottoms are there before Your hand of mercy reaches down to save? How much more can You take away from me when I already have nothing left? Where is the beauty from ashes You promised? I'm waiting, praying, seeking Your salvation. Don't delay any longer, Lord! Yet I know somehow Your timing is perfect, and Your ways are higher than my own.

[I know you are probably thinking, *Wow! She sounds like Job whining to God*. Yes, I felt like him many times throughout this valley. But then as always, I opened my Bible and the Lord spoke directly to my cry once again: *They were at their wits' end. Then they cried out to the Lord in their trouble, and he brought them out of their distress* (Psalm 107:27–28 NIV). And also, *Sarah became pregnant and bore a son to Abraham in his old age, at the very time God had promised him* (Genesis 21:2 NIV). God was telling me that although I was at my wits' end, His timing for the answer would be perfect.]

MAY 31, 2023

Lord, is it a sin to say I hate my life right now? There is so much darkness and so many trials surrounding me on every side. My older daughter is having serious health concerns, and the doctors can't figure it out. She is in Texas, and I cannot be there for her. Minnie's addiction is so bad that she is stealing from me to feed it. My husband works so late I feel alone, and even my dogs wake me up all night with problems of their own. I'm exhausted mentally and emotionally from the countless hours on the phone trying to get Minnie help, and I'm worn out trying to keep her alive long enough to get her into a facility. My body is broken, probably because my spirit it broken. I can't even look forward to vacation time because Minnie will be away and I might need to fly home and get her. I'm shaking and can barely breathe—but You say to trust You, that this is somehow for my good, that You will restore—it's hard to see right now. How much more do You require of me?

JUNE 2, 2023

Lord, it's just like You to lead us in a way that is exactly opposite of how I would have gone. I've been fighting so hard to get Minnie to the facility I wanted her to be in, yet all along You know I've been praying for You to shut all other doors but the right one. Well, all the doors I loved slammed shut and the one I never would have chosen is wide open—the one of which I said definitely *no* as soon as I talked to the person on the phone. There were many reasons for this, but I won't get into them here. It kills me—absolutely kills me—to send her there, but that is the *one* door You opened. You made it clear to me that You want her at this facility, and although I don't understand it, I have to trust You. As my friend told me, "She will be bathed in prayer the whole time." Lord, You can use even a donkey to bring about Your purpose (Numbers 22), so I know You can use this place and the people You have there. My prayer all along has been "Do what You need to do to rescue her and heal her," and only You know the end from the beginning and know just what she needs for You to accomplish that in her life. My baby is in Your hands, and I say again: You love her more than I ever could.

JUNE 6, 2023

Lord, I've placed all my trust in You, walked the way You would have me go, even though everything inside me said *no*. I've placed Minnie in Your hands, trusting You to do what she needs . . . so why, why, why would You allow them to place [that person] in the room with Minnie? How do I know if I'm actually hearing from You? Am I actually following Your leading? My heart and my mind are broken and empty. I'm trying to leave this in Your hands, but I can't imagine this is Your plan. How can I know? . . . Wow! I placed my pen down and picked up the printout of the blog I quoted before, and there the words jumped off the page: "Do not be afraid or discouraged because of this vast army. For the battle is not yours but God's. Stand firm, hold your position, and see the salvation of the Lord on your behalf" (2 Chronicles 20:15–17 NIV). There is a vast army of evil coming against her, but this is *Your* battle! I will stand firm and see the salvation of the Lord on Minnie's behalf. *That* is how You speak to me! I can know without a doubt that this is from You and the victory is Yours. . . . Oh, my goodness! I finished writing and went to read the Bible, and my reading today took me to the same exact passage!

JUNE 8, 2023

If a person allows it, he can find something at every turn of the road that will rob him of his victory and his peace of mind. . . . God is still on His throne, and He can turn defeat into victory in a split second, if we will only trust Him (quoted in Cowman 225).

[Oh, how I needed this reminder! Oh, how I need this reminder every single day! "For He Himself has said, 'I will never leave you nor forsake you.' So we may boldly say: 'The Lord is my helper; I will not fear'" (Hebrews 13:5–6).]

JUNE 13, 2023

Well, Lord, it's been quite a week. From Minnie sobbing and begging to come home every night . . . to me finally letting her know I cannot take her home . . . to her being so mad she hung up and didn't want to see us or talk to us . . . to a huge breakthrough! We went to see her this morning for the first time since we dropped her off, and she's finally coming back to life. She's eating and enjoying food; she's actually getting hungry. She is off weed and nicotine, and her smile is back. Lord, continue the healing until it's physical, emotional, mental, and most of all, spiritual. I read again yesterday Your promise that I would see the goodness of the Lord in the land of the living, and You keep sending me butterflies as a reminder of that promise. I shared that with Minnie and she spotted some butterflies of her own today too and was happy to tell me about it. Keep working, Lord!

JUNE 15, 2023

Lord, Minnie is doing a little better every day now, but it's hard for me to get so excited because I know there is a lot of work to be done, and the closer we get to vacation the more and more sad I become. I planned this trip around her, and it could be our last. But also I have this sense of something she is holding back—a secret sin, someone she was seeing before going into the facility. I don't know but I also know I can't worry. You can get to the heart of all her problems, and I know Your Word does not return void (Isaiah 55:11), and all the truth we spoke into her life as a child will surface one day and she will remember and call on You and throw aside all the evil from this world—in Jesus's name!

[A few weeks before Jesus took her, I asked her about this and she told confirmed what I knew in my spirit. In fact, she started facing the situation, and I believe this was part of the reason she began to spiral again. It dug up all the horrible memories and a potential confrontation and legal battle.]

JUNE 17, 2023

Lord, as You know, since Minnie has been away I've been praying that You would send me reminders of Your promise to me for her healing and salvation—I asked You to send me butterflies as Your reminder, and You have shown up in big ways each day! You have sent actual butterflies across my path, even in the strangest places; you've sent them in the form of a gift for my birthday, and even in car sunshade. Since I told Minnie about my prayer, now even she is seeing them everywhere too! Let it be a reminder to her too, that there is a promise over her life. Lord, keep moving, keep reminding, keep loving, as only You can do. The only thing I want for my birthday is her healing and salvation. I prayed it, You promised it, I believe it, and I thank You in advance for it!

JUNE 21, 2023

Lord, I got to see my girl yesterday, and she looked so happy and beautiful, and my heart is rejoicing. Then today I got a call from her therapist saying insurance wants to discharge her! She is not ready! We are not ready! But You know—You know when she needs to come home and why—Your timing is perfect every single time. You know the ending before the beginning, and I know You are working all things out. I don't want her home even a second before You want her home, and You know how to work this, even with our vacation too. I'm at the place of total surrender, and I will not worry. This is Your problem, not mine, and I know Your plan is perfect!

JUNE 25, 2023

Well, Lord, as always, You do things completely unexpected, yet Your timing is always perfect. Minnie's insurance decided to stop paying, so two days ago I had to go pick her up. Was it what I wanted? *No!* Was it enough time for her? In my eyes, no! Was the timing perfect? In Your eyes, yes! So now here I am with my girl, and although she got some important tools, I know she has a long way to go, and I'm like a deer in the headlights. However, she is happy to be home, and she is taking charge of her food and her schedule—but I also know I can't leave her alone for a while, so I'm home from church sitting with her. I trust You're going to keep moving in her life. It seems she's just farther from You now after being there with all the self-help stuff. She said something today that was like a knife in my heart. She said, "When *you* get to heaven . . ." and the way she said it, she meant only me. Lord, You sure have a lot of work to do, but it's a job only You can do. You're my only hope for her—help her to see You are her only hope. Cause her to become disillusioned with this world and with sin. Help her to recognize the lies of the enemy and to stop deceiving herself, and pour out Your Spirit on the whole family. Help me to remember that You love her more than I ever could, and You are setting things in place for her to eventually come back to You. Your reminders of the promise over her life are everywhere. What a glorious day that will be! Your word in her life will not return void. I thank You in advance. Your promise is as good as cash in my hand.

JUNE 28, 2023

Lord, it surely didn't take long for her to go right back to where she was before, isolating herself in her room all day, being short-tempered and moody, and even going back to her drugs. Lord, my head is spinning because it's too much for me; I can't have her here because I can't do anything and I don't want that in my house. Do I kick her out? Do I let her continue to walk all over me? I don't know what to do, but my eyes are on You. My heart is so heavy, my eyes are worn out from crying, and my mind is always spinning. I worry, pray, try not to worry, pray, cry, ask for help, say I believe, and then I worry more—Lord, please help!

JUNE 29, 2023

Lord, I've had a lot of very hard days, but I feel this is right up there in my top three; I can't even pray. I'm thankful for the prayers of those around me holding me up, and I'm more than thankful You are at the throne interceding for me. I'm empty, broken, totally wrecked, and I don't know what to do. I feel like Peter looking at the storm beneath his feet and sinking (Mark 14). I try to look to You, but then another wave comes over me. I feel as though I am barely holding on. I've cried more today than I can remember. I have chest pains and it's hard to breathe. I'm losing myself; I'm just a shell of who I was—so empty. Please fill me with Your Spirit in place of the emptiness. I have nothing left.

JULY 5, 2023

"Therefore, behold, I will allure her, will bring her into the wilderness, and speak comfort to her. I will give her her vineyard from there, and the Valley of Achor [Achor *means 'Trouble'*] *as a door of hope; she*

shall sing there, as in the days of her youth, as in the day when she came up from the land of Egypt" (Hosea 2:14–15).

[I had read this passage over and over and wrote notes in the margin every single time I read it. I could see how the Lord was doing just this in Minnie's life, allowing her to be allured into the wilderness until total hopelessness (achor, trouble) would overtake her, and *then* He could speak tenderly to her and lead her through the door of hope. I obviously didn't know it all the years I had read this, that the door of hope would ultimately be the door into eternity, but I can say now that she is certainly singing as in the days of her youth.]

JULY 17, 2023

> *For the Lord said to me, "I will take My rest, and I will look from My dwelling place"* (Isaiah 18:4). (This passage describes the Lord just looking on from heaven as Ethiopia was invaded. It seemed He was silent and uninvolved.) "Yet His silence is not to be confused with passive agreement or consent. He is simply biding His time and will arise at the most opportune moment, just when the plans of the wicked are on the verge of success, in order to overwhelm the enemy with disaster. (Jesus slept while His apostles feared for their lives in the raging storm.) Also, when Jesus heard Lazarus was sick, He delayed going to him for several days. Do these stories show that Jesus really doesn't care about what happens to us? No! *Jesus was simply waiting for the perfect moment when He could intercede most effectively. Is the Lord being quiet with you? Nevertheless,*

He is attentive and still sees everything . . . and He will come to save you when the perfect moment has arrived."
(Cowman 276)

[Wow! Looking back at this devotional, I again see how Jesus's delay in saving Minnie until the exact perfect moment was to show His glory, overwhelm the enemy, and intercede most effectively, just as He did when He calmed the deadly storm and raised Lazarus from the dead. Also, in the story of Lazarus it's important to see that it began with how Jesus loved Mary, Martha, and Lazarus in John 11:5. We see that His motivation, even in the delay, was and always is love.]

JULY 22, 2023

Lord, as always Your timing is perfect. The day we left for our trip, I was making calls to see where we could leave Minnie while we were gone. It was one of the lowest, most difficult moments of my life (Little did I know just how much worse it would get in the coming months). But You knew she needed to get out of that treatment facility and to be with us on vacation. I'm sitting here on our last morning, reflecting on Your goodness and the healing that has happened on this trip. You knew this is what needed to happen, not just time with us (and especially her sister) but also time with Papa and Nana too. Yes, there were some hard moments where she was in a deep funk, but You pulled her out each time. This was a very special time together, and it's bittersweet knowing we all have reality to face.

[Looking back, I see that this was the most important and the last trip we ever took together, and God knew it needed to happen, which is why He caused her early release from the treatment center. Minnie and I had planned this trip together. We mapped out all of her favorite places to revisit and things to do: Glacier National Park,

Leavenworth, crabbing in Waldport, the stunning seaside in Yachats, dune buggies in Florence, and waterskiing on Lake Shasta. It was a perfect trip, ending with the most brilliant sunset in Solvang as the sun set on our last trip together.]

JULY 25, 2023

Lord, we've been home for two nights and You see everything she's doing—the insane nighttime binging (just not purging anymore) the "hanging out with friends," the taking $100 cash out of her account—all the things she's done before. But this time what will be different is *me*. Lord, all I can do is give her to You in prayer and wait on You to tell me what to do, what to say, and when to keep my mouth shut. I know there is no treatment plan that can heal her—it's only You! And I pray that You don't delay anymore (although I want Your will and Your perfect timing, because I know that will yield the perfect healing, the perfect blessings, and all the glory to You). Help keep me and all of us strong while we wait on You, Lord.

JULY 28, 2023

Lord, back and forth, up and down, high and low—as Minnie has gone, my heart has gone, but I don't want it to be that way. Lord, help my heart to remain steadfast, trusting in You. When there are no answers, help me remember that You are the answer. Help me remember that the best and only thing I can do for her is pray. Lord, I pray that You would transform her by the renewing of her mind. Give her hope and direction for her future. Lord, You are my only hope and You've brought me through the fire before, so I know You will do it again because Your promises are yes and amen. Draw her to You like never before. Put an unquenchable thirst in her heart for Your living water.

JULY 30, 2023

Lord, You are good no matter what is happening around me. I will worship You for who You are, not because of what I hope and pray for—yet part of who You are is Your being a promise keeper! You have given me many promises for my Minnie, so I praise You that You will keep those promises. You tell me in Romans 4:17 that You give life to the dead and that You call those things that do not exist as though they did (You call her chosen, beautiful, worthy, a soul worth saving, the one for whom You leave the ninety-nine to seek and save)—so because You have said this, I believe it, and I long to see it happen just as You said. "Donna, against all hope, in hope believed." Your promises through Jesus Christ and by His blood are yes and amen!

AUGUST 2, 2023

Lord, You see how it's going, so I don't even need to tell You, and when things are bad my normal instinct is to overthink, overact, overdo trying to figure it out, overwatch her, and overdo trying to control the situation—all while going crazy and making things worse. Lord, You're doing a work in me because I really am just trying to release it all to You. I can trust the one who died for me! Every time I want to tell her something, Your Spirit has put His hand over my mouth. There is so much I want to call her out on, but I pray You would convict and guide her. You are in every detail of this and I keep reminding myself that You love her more than I ever could. Help *her* to know that and to respond to Your love. I either trust who You are or I don't—I either trust Your promises or I don't—I either believe You can do it or I don't.

AUGUST 6, 2023

Lord, today in church I learned the Greek meaning of the word *sufferings*: crushing emotions, layered pressures of life—well, I am definitely suffering, as You said we would. But You said our suffering is never for nothing. I know You're working something greater in me, through me, and in this situation, although right now it seems hopeless. I'm worn out from the battle, and I'm crushed emotionally from how she has treated me through it all. I know I can't expect her to show love to me when she doesn't love herself—but, God, it's destroying me. I want to give up, but I can never do that—for her sake and because You told me not to. So I hold on . . . barely. Waiting, praying, hoping, expecting.

AUGUST 8, 2023

Lord, You see the doors slammed shut on us once again—doors that looked wide open. You see all my emotions, so raw, as if I was sucker-punched and got the wind knocked out of me. And I see Minnie's hope for help just crumble. I sit here and say, "I trust You and I want Your will," but then this happens and I go into panic mode. Then You gently remind me again that somehow You're working it out, that my hope is in You alone and not in a facility. God, if she would just open her heart to You, she would see that You alone are the answer. God, how much longer does she have to suffer—how much longer do *I* have to suffer? Keep reminding me of Your promises; don't ever leave me alone, God. Where would I be without You? Please lead me every step of the way and help me not to lose heart—the morning is coming!

[I was making calls all day for several days, trying to get Minnie into another facility. I knew she needed more help immediately. She got accepted into one, but at the last second they said the insurance pulled out. It was a roller coaster of emotions.]

AUGUST 11, 2023

God, this was the worst night of my life, hands down (Again, this was just a precursor to what would happen just three months later. It was this night, her eighteenth birthday, she ran away to go be with "the boy" once again, in spite of all of us begging her not to leave. She packed a backpack and took off). How can I even put into words what I'm feeling? Anger, worry, abandonment, confusion, the most extreme sadness I could have ever imagined, questioning, second-guessing—yet trying to remember all You've been telling me, Your promises (and how the last few days the massive butterflies have been circling our yard), yet empty and alone—but still all the Scriptures You wrote to me come to mind . . . so many promises; help me to remember, to focus on You, who You are, what You've done, and what You said You will do. I've prayed all along for Your will, Your timing, for You to do what only You can do, to send her what she needs. Lord, I know that none of the things I've done, or the medications, or the facilities, or the therapy, could ever heal her, and maybe I've been trying to fix what only You can. I suppose if those things helped, she would never be able to feel the sting of sin and never hit the bottom in order for her to finally look up. I've thought many times (and so has she) that "this must be the bottom," but then she goes right back to it. I guess if this stuff could help then it wouldn't be a miracle and You wouldn't get the glory. Lord, I know You have worked miracles way more miraculous than this. You pushed back the sea, made the sun stand still, defeated armies with a word, made a donkey speak Your truth, raised Lazarus from the dead, healed the demon-possessed, and defeated death—so why would You fail now? You can't fail! You are the God of the universe and the God who leaves the ninety-nine to save the one. You are the Lord of heaven's armies, so I pray now You would send Your biggest, baddest angels to surround and protect Minnie until You break through to her. In the name of Jesus, break the demonic hold on her life, however You have to do it (and there it was—He finally did it how He had to do it once and for all)! Help me to live in faith and not fear! Help those friends around me see how I handle this—in prayer, hope, and faith—and let that be what finally draws them to You. I've been praying so long for them specifically. Lord, let these souls be saved through all of this. Let those around me see my faith and Your miracles! I need You to do what truly only You can do! "I would have lost heart unless I had believed that I would see the goodness of the Lord in the land of the living. Wait on the lord; Be of good courage, and He shall strength your heart; wait, I say, on the Lord!" (Psalm 27:13–14).

[Then, as usual, I opened my devotional and read Habakkuk 3:17–18, which reads, "Though the fig tree does not bud and there are no grapes on the vines, though the olive crop fails and the fields produce no food, though there are no sheep in the pen ad no cattle in the stalls, *yet I will rejoice in the Lord, I will be joyful in God my Savior*" (NIV, emphasis added). It was an absolute disastrous situation described in this passage. Everything of value in the prophet's life was gone—yet he rejoiced in the Lord!

> Blessed assurance! Salvation is coming from Him. It is on the way. It will come from Him and from no one else. He will have all the glory of it, for He alone can and will perform it, and He will perform it most certainly in His own time and manner. He will save from doubt, suffering, slander, and distress. Although we see no sign of it as yet, we are satisfied to wait for the Lord's will, for we have no doubt about His love and faithfulness. He will make certain work of it before long, and we will praise Him at once for the coming mercy. (Spurgeon 235)

AUGUST 12, 2023

One daughter has left again for school; another one is living on the street with *him*—pain so deep that I can hardly move. I want him gone forever so he can't hurt her anymore—or You could save him. Wouldn't that be something? You say nothing we could ever do is too bad that You can't forgive. If he won't accept You, get him out of her life forever and break the demonic spell she is under! God, no one has the answers but You. Lead me, guide me, let me shut out all the voices but Yours. Comfort my family and me. Bring salvation and healing in ways only You can do—exceedingly, abundantly, more than I can ask or imagine.

[Turning to my devotional, I read 2 Peter 1:4: "He has given us his very great and precious promises" (NIV). And from Charles H. Spurgeon, "When a shipbuilder erects a boat . . . he builds it to sail the seas and to weather the storms. . . . When He gave you promises and asked you to trust them, He made His promises suitable for times of storms and high seas" (quoted in Cowman 308). Despite the fact that taking her out of this world is not how I ever imagined God would save her, He definitely answered my prayer. I had asked for God to remove the boy forever to break the demonic hold. God indeed answered this prayer, even though it is never what I imagined.]

AUGUST 16, 2023

Lord, how can I even wrap my head around all that has happened? There really are no words to describe all the emotions, all the pain and heartache, the highs and lows, the questioning why, the waiting, the hope, the hope crashing down—but when I finally entered Your sanctuary with a sacrifice of praise this week, You renewed my hope and restored my spirit. I got to hold my baby again yesterday, a girl battered and broken—but safe! Lord, You see it all, You know who she is and where she has been and what she has done, but when she calls on Jesus, all You will see is His blood that has washed her white as snow. Lord, I thank You for how You used my son with his love and boldness for You to speak truth into her life. Your Word does not return void. I am still waiting for the big breakthrough, but I am thankful for You bringing her out of the hell she was in.

[Minnie escaped "the boy" at two o'clock in the morning and walked miles through gang-infested city areas to get back to our town. We got her into a hotel the next day because I knew I couldn't have her just come home until I figured out what to do. When I got her there, she didn't want me to leave. She just fell back on the bed and started weeping. I would have given anything to hold onto her at that moment and never let her go. She started unpacking her backpack and I saw my son's Bible! I asked her about it and she said, with a tear in her eye, the night she left he had walked into her room and given it to her, and he wrote a note in it for her. Oh, how the Lord used him and his example in her life! She always told me how good he is and how she hated when he saw her do things she knew she shouldn't be doing. She loved and respected him so much, and I know this Bible meant the world to her.]

AUGUST 17, 2023

Lord, how I wish You would just come tell me what to do as You did with the Old Testament prophets. I feel as if I am tossed back and forth by the raging storm, and I am crying out for You to wake up and say, "Peace, be still!" But then You reprimanded the apostles because they had "little faith." I feel like I have faith—I am waiting in hopeful expectation for You to work a wondrous miracle, but then another wave comes and knocks me back under until I can't breathe again. I don't know what to do, but my eyes are on You. Help me to not keep trying to figure things out or solve this because I could never help her the way You can. Your healing is complete and it's once and for all. God, I pray once again for You to open the one door for us to go through, and continue slamming shut all the others that look good but that You know are not where she should be—and give me strength and peace to accept it.

AUGUST 20, 2023

Lord, I am learning so much from unlikely places. My friend sent me a podcast he and his wife recorded, and he said what I've stated here many times about myself—he said that he always had faith in You, but when there was no way out, he *had* to trust You. Whoa! Of course I have faith in who You are, and I know Your promises are true, and I know You use all things for our good—but now that I have nothing left in this world to help me, do I trust that You will do all You have said? And when people have asked me how do I do it, I've always just said, "I wake up each day, so I don't have a choice." But my friend's wife said something that hit me—"I get out of bed because of hope." Lord, as I walk through this valley of the shadow of death, let me remember that You didn't extinguish the fire for the Hebrew young men . . . because You are Lord *over* the fire! (Rogers, 2021)

[And then my reading in my devotional spoke to me again: "If God has called us to His highest and best, each of us will have a time of crisis, when all our resources will fail and when we face either ruin or something better than we have ever dreamed. But before we can receive the blessing, we must rely on God's infinite help. We must be willing to let go, surrendering completely to Him, and cease from our own wisdom, strength, and righteousness. . . . God knows how to lead us to the point of crisis, and He knows how to lead us through it" (Cowman 319).]

AUGUST 23, 2023

Lord, today is Minnie's last day at my sister's house. (Our friend and my sister's family took Minnie in for us to just try to reset her and get her going on the right path again. She loved her time in both places, and God really used them to speak into her life after she had been so badly damaged. I'm forever grateful for their willing hearts, and I also think it was this time spent with them that made her passing hit them so much harder too.) I have so many emotions. I love how well she is doing, and I'm so afraid of her coming home because of how that has gone in the past—when she lived with her friend for a week and then came home; when she went to the facility and then came home; when we went on vacation and then came home—I guess it's the letdown or all the triggers coming home after being away. Yet I'm thankful for another chance, and I'm hopeful and trusting You that You are putting all the pieces together. I've said so many times over and over this past year or more that I'm done, that I can't do it anymore. Well, Lord, I truly am done, and I can't do it anymore—*but God!* I'm actually so hopeful! I'm so ready to see Your salvation!

AUGUST 24, 2023

Lord, today is the day Minnie comes home, and You see everything in my heart and mind. Let this be her "prodigal returns" moment, never to leave again! I'm so thankful for the support team You have placed around me, especially my sister. She is the truly the best friend I've ever had. Thank You for the praying friends who continue lifting us up daily. Thank You, Jesus, for continuously interceding for us before the throne of the Father. Through all this pain and suffering I've never doubted Your goodness and love, even through the questioning "why." Help me to remain in gratitude through whatever happens next—I leave it in Your hands.

[The first thing Minnie wanted to do when she got home was go to Joseph's football game. She became his biggest fan, coming with me to every game, wearing school gear, cheering the most loudly, and tackle-hugging him after the games. She adored her brother, and she was so proud of him and happy to support him. Even though I could never have imagined what would happen next, the Lord has answered this very specific prayer, and somehow He truly has kept me in gratitude. It truly is unexplainable.]

AUGUST 29, 2023

Lord, today I am taking Minnie (who is very willing to go) to a lady who has a deliverance ministry so she can pray over her. I've been fasting and remaining in a spirit of prayer for several days. Lord, I'm trusting You for a mighty work in her life in the name of Jesus! Break her bondage and let her finally call on You, Lord. Let her see You, feel You, know You. Lord, save her! Our time here is short and Your promise is that I would see Your goodness in the land of the living, and I have felt that part of it would be that I would see her decision to get baptized! I'm anticipating, hoping, praying, and expecting, but ultimately knowing it's Your timing I wait for.

[Looking back, I don't know if this was good or not. I feel that maybe I was seeking more help from others instead of just laying her in the hands of Jesus, the only one who can deliver. I truly feel that I often reacted to things like the Israelites, who would always look to Egypt or others for help instead of going straight to God.]

AUGUST 30, 2023

My God, You know what was said in the two hours Minnie was with the lady yesterday. She didn't tell me much except most of the time was just talking, I think just peeling off the layers. When she got out, she had a peace about her. I wish I knew what happened, but You know. All I can say is that later she went to hang out with her friends, and when she got home she said they all talked about it and they want to get baptized by Pastor Jack! Lord, again You know her heart and You also know this has been my prayer from the beginning. Now I pray against all the demonic forces that would try to steal her away—in Jesus's name they can't have her!

[Well, she did decide to get baptized, but I never saw it happen. It's like what Jesus warned in Matthew 12: if you sweep a house clean of a demonic presence and leave it empty (rather than immediately filling it with Jesus), the same spirit will come back and bring his "thug spirit friends" with him. I told her many times that she was oppressed on all sides by demons. She would get mad and say I think she's possessed. No, someone who gave her heart to Jesus cannot be possessed but she can be oppressed, and she surely was! In fact, it was about this time that she was given a diagnosis of borderline personality disorder (BPD), and then it all started making sense to me. I believe demonic oppression can represent itself as mental health disorders, and she now was said to have anxiety, depression, and BPD. When I think of the constant torment my poor baby was in, my heart shatters. It's as if she truly could not make rational decisions, or if she did, it wouldn't last long. She always wanted to do what was right (we talked about it all the time, how she wanted to settle down with a good man someday and have a quiet, normal, happy life), but then she would allude to the fact that she makes careless and impulsive decisions all the time. This was the BPD in her life, and this is what would soon take her life.]

AUGUST 31, 2023

Lord, You know the lies and deception and doubt the enemy is feeding into Minnie; he is afraid because he knows he is losing his grip on her, so he is working overtime—but in the name of Jesus, he cannot have her! I don't care what she said yesterday. (She asked how she could believe that God could forgive someone after that person has hurt so many people. She was watching the Dahmer documentary and we were talking about how he became a Christian. She couldn't wrap her head around believing in a God who would forgive him and not punish him. I think because she had been so damaged by so many people, she wanted to believe they could not be forgiven.) I trust You, and she will be saved! You've promised, and

I believe it, even though my eyes cannot see it. Satan has lied to her long enough! Lord, break through so she can see Your truth. Block the lies from the enemy. It's time to claim this victory! I believe, I trust, and I thank You for it now!

SEPTEMBER 3, 2023

Lord, another Sunday when Minnie said she would come to church and she didn't, but I will not get discouraged this time—I will pray with even greater faith and not fear. Satan is working hard to keep his grip on her because, Lord, he knows You are breaking through. I don't care anymore what I see with my eyes because I have brought her to Your throne, knowing that it is the best place for her to be, where Jesus is making intercession for her even now. Lord, cause her to become more and more disgusted with the evil she sees in this world and to become disillusioned with sin. Break the bondage that has her in captivity so her mind can be free. Help her to stop deceiving herself and others so Your truth can shine brightly to her. May she bow her prideful knee before You, King Jesus!

SEPTEMBER 8, 2023

Lord, I was looking through my old Bible and there I found my promise to You on 9/17/21 that I would fast and pray for Minnie every Monday until I see her return to You. Here I am two years later, still fasting and praying and waiting. "I would have lost heart if I didn't know I would see the goodness of the Lord in the land of the living." My prayers are different now, as You've tested and stretched my faith these last two years, but the heart of them remains the same—save and heal my daughter! May she turn back to You! You can do it in Your own awesome way, whether she cracks open her Bible, steps foot in church again, hears my words about You (or not)—You have amazing ways of crashing into the world of those who are lost until they have no choice but to call on You. That is my prayer!

[Wow! Looking back at how my prayers changed over time into total dependence on God to do it however He needed to do it, I believe He was waiting for me to get to this point so He could save and heal her according to *His* will and not my own. I always prayed for His will, and I would tell God that I know I'm aligned with His will because we both wanted Minnie's salvation—however, it wasn't until I submitted and aligned my will with His *"how"* that I released Him to do what needed to be done to accomplish the *"what."*]

SEPTEMBER 14, 2023

Lord, You know our time we have left is short; the signs are everywhere, but ultimately You know the day and the hour and You know what needs to happen to save my girl, so what else can I do but trust You? There is no one and nothing else I can trust in. You're already there—and You're timeless, so of course You aren't worried because You've already seen her salvation. Yet You tell me to pray without ceasing. Why? I think it's to get *me* closer to You as I learn to trust in a way I've never known before so I too can say with all my heart, "It is well with my soul."

[Exactly two months later this would ultimately be tested. As I look back on this now, and not realizing I had prayed this exact prayer, that is one of the songs we picked for Minnie's service. I not only see how the Lord answered my biggest prayer, but I also see now how He worked all of the little details together as well. What love! What reassurance that He heard every single prayer I prayed—I am in awe of His lovingkindness to me!]

SEPTEMBER 15, 2023

Lord—my God whom I serve is able to deliver Minnie from the fiery furnace. *But if not* . . . Tomorrow is the day of our church baptism, the day I've prayed and fasted for, believed for and am still holding out hope for, but Lord, I know You are never late. You are always perfectly on time. When I try to pick fruit before it's ripe, it is hard and bitter, but when I allow You to ripen the fruit, it is sweet and delicious. What can I do but trust Your timing? That is all I can do, all I want to do, and all I need to do. "Stand firm, hold your position, and see the salvation of the Lord on your behalf."

SEPTEMBER 17, 2023

Lord, yesterday came and went, and my eyes tell me nothing changed in her heart. I'm going to be honest—I feel let down because I believed I would see her baptized yesterday. Do I not have faith even the size of a mustard seed? Lord, I believe and have not waivered, so why did You answer the prophets when they asked in faith, yet here I am still waiting, trying to massage my broken heart? The message at church this morning was for me—having a loyal heart toward You throughout all my life and all my circumstances. The passage was about Asa and how You wanted to bestow on him a greater blessing, but because he tried to solve his own problem without You, he missed out on what You had for him. Loyalty is a lifetime of daily choices, so I choose now that my heart is steadfast in spite of my seemingly unanswered prayers—but Your purpose is to show Yourself strong for Your glory!

[This speaks volumes about the importance of going to church! If I allowed my broken heart to stop me from going, I would have missed out on the message God had for me.]

SEPTEMBER 20, 2023

"Since the beginning of the world men have not heard nor perceived by the ear, nor has the eye seen any God besides You, who acts for the one who waits for Him" (Isaiah 64:4). Lord, what does this mean for me? It means that if I continue to wait—truly wait—

on You (without all my trying to figure things out, all my mental gymnastics trying to make the pieces fit, all my trying to speed along Your promises, much as Abraham did), You will act on my behalf! I know it is going to be very different than anything I would have planned, and that's the beauty of it — You will get the glory and no one else, because my prayer from the beginning was and still is that You would use this for Minnie's good, Your glory, and for the salvation of many!

[Reading this again was very difficult, yet at the same time it was very comforting. I see how the Lord took me on this journey to prepare my heart, to get to the point where I trusted Him not only with the process but also the outcome, knowing full well that He would answer my prayer!]

SEPTEMBER 24, 2023

> *God is most glorified in the hardest redemptive circumstances* (Pastor Jack Hibbs, Hibbs 2023).

Lord, what can I do but pray that Your Spirit draws her into repentance? I can't live in fear over it anymore. I know You're doing the work, and I don't have to, nor is there anything I can do. There is so much more to her story—You're not done with her yet! You have always been faithful and You will be again.

SEPTEMBER 27, 2023

> "You will light my lamp" (Psalm 18:28). *The mercy is that if God lights the candle, no one can blow it out, and it cannot burn itself out. The lights that the Lord kindled in the beginning are still shining. The Lord's lamps may need trimming at times, but He does not put them out* (Spurgeon 283).

[As a child Minnie loved Jesus and proclaimed her belief in Him. This is my reassurance! As you read through these journal entries, many times you see me praying for Minnie's salvation. Since her death, the Lord has spoken to me through some amazing pastors and teachers about what salvation truly means and what it doesn't. Most instrumental in my newfound reassurance of her salvation has been not only Pastor Jack Hibbs but also Dr. J. B. Hixon. His main area of study is soteriology, or the doctrine of salvation. He often quotes Titus 3:5: "Not by works of righteousness which we have done, but according to His mercy He saved us." Repeatedly he drives home the difference between positional righteousness versus practical righteousness. Positional righteousness is the moment of salvation, in which our position in Christ is secure for eternity. This is once and for all, never to be undone by anything we could do. However, practical righteousness refers to our relationship or fellowship with the Lord, that our "joy may be full" (John 15:11). The moment Minnie trusted Jesus for salvation as a child, she was eternally positionally secure in Him. Her actions separated her from fellowship with Him and the joy of the Lord, but it could not change the *fact* that she was sealed for eternity! (Hixson, 2024)]

SEPTEMBER 30, 2023

Lord, how much more can my heart take? The lies, the disrespect, the meaningless "I love you's" followed by more lies. Of course, I love my girl so much it hurts, but she has shattered me so badly time and time again, I just can't take it anymore. God, I've tried to keep my heart steadfast, but the human me just asks, "Do You even care? Are You listening? Can I trust You? Why should I even pray when every prayer is met with more and more trouble and hurt?" The soul of me connected to You says, "I can trust You and Your promises. I don't have to worry. You are working all things for my good." Part of me wants her to just go and stop torturing me. The mother side of me wants her to stay so I can protect and take care of her. All of me is hurting and needing You more than ever.

[Minnie had just started seeing a new boy. For the first time in her life she was finally treated right. She said to me, "Even if we don't end up together, I have to thank him for showing me how I should be treated." He was a Marine and a kind and respectful young man. After just a few dates, they were already talking about a future. The problem was not with him. The problem was with her. She just could not tell me the truth, always hiding what she was doing. I had been so beaten down by all her lies and I thought we were moving forward, so this really sent me reeling. I was so happy that she found a wonderful young man, yet I just never knew what each day would bring with her.]

OCTOBER 1, 2023

Lord, I've felt it before and here it comes again—pain so deep that I can hardly move. The endless cycle of—Minnie gets into trouble. Minnie calls me to rescue her. Minnie loves me and clings to me. Minnie starts lying and sneaking around again. Minnie "hates" me and makes a brash move . . . and so the cycle repeats. We're currently in the hates me/brash move stage, the part where she tells everyone how horrible I am and that I am mentally ill, the part where I throw up my hands, pull away, and tell You I want her out and I just wait for the next shoe to drop, the part where I freak out and tell You just to take control (until I take it all back upon me again); the part where I question You and Your promises and then resolve to trust You no matter what (until the "what" happens). Lord, make my heart steadfast! Show me the way; give me wisdom—I truly don't know what to do at all anymore.

[Out of nowhere as I was away from the house this day and then returned to an empty house, I checked Minnie's location, and she was at the Army recruiting office. I knew at that moment that she went to sign up. Remember—she was on so many different medications for her mental health, and she decided to quit them all cold turkey! Of course, she took my questioning as a personal attack and unloaded so much filth on me. I stopped and prayed, and with the Lord's prompting on my heart, I gently went into her room after some time had passed and I just told her, "I think it's a good idea for you to join." She was shocked and probably a bit upset that her plan to upset me did not work. I helped her devise a plan to get herself ready to go take the exams shortly after. She studied day and night, worked out hard, went for long runs, but I think in her heart she knew she was not cut out for it. She never expressed her fears to me because she knew she had to follow through to prove a point. I'm glad I showed her support during this time. I think she needed that more than anything.

OCTOBER 3, 2023

> *"In the multitude of my anxieties within me, Your comforts delight my soul" (Psalm 94:19). Lord, You know all my anxious thoughts, and there are many right now. Yet You tell me over and over not to be anxious about anything but to present all of it before You with prayers, supplication, and thanksgiving, and Your peace that passes all understanding will guard my heart and my mind—so I'm bringing it all to You and leaving it at Your feet, and I will be thankful for the blessings upon blessings You have given me—first and foremost, my own salvation, without which I would be lost, dying, angry, hopeless, helpless. You've always provided, even throughout the hardest times. You give me hope against all hope. Though this life is uncertain, my future is secure, and my biggest prayer is that You would bring that same hope to my Minnie—I still wait for Your*

promise. "Therefore if you desire to know God's voice, never consider the final outcome or the possible results" (quoted in Cowman 374).

OCTOBER 5, 2023

"Some time later the brook dried up" (1 Kings 17:7 NIV). The education of our faith is incomplete if we have yet to learn that God's providence works through loss . . . and that He gives the gift of emptiness. . . . One way or the other, we must all learn the difference between trusting in the gift and trusting in the Giver. The gift may last for a season, but the Giver is the only eternal love. . . . And whenever our earthly stream or any other outer resource has dried up, it has been allowed so we may learn that our hope and help are in God, who made heaven and earth (quoted in Cowman 376).

[I realize that too often I seek the gift and not the Giver. His gifts are just a manifestation of His great love for us, so shouldn't I seek only Him? My brook has now run dry, but my promise is not from the brook but from the one who made the brook.]

OCTOBER 26, 2023

Lord, You see the mundane—both in her and in me. I guess it's good that there is no crisis going on with her, but it also wearies me—the day in, day out, with no change in her heart. Yet I know that You can use even the mundane to reach her. You can come to her in a thought or a dream; You can even visit her in a vision. I've always imagined her returning to You would come as a result of one of her many crises, but sometimes You come to us not in the thunder, the storm, or the hurricane but in a small whisper, so our only choice is to draw near to hear You. Lord, help me not to become weary; help my unbelief. Help me never to forsake the solitude of Your presence. I need You more than ever—and so does she. Hannah Whitall Smith stated, "You may not see or feel the inner workings of His silent power, but rest assured it is always mightily at work" (quoted in Cowman 406).

[Minnie went to take her Army recruiting exam several days prior. I prayed with her before she left that the Lord's will would be done for her life. She returned shortly after; the recruiter had seen the large scar on her forearm and immediately disqualified her for mental health reasons. She was so dejected but also maybe slightly relieved. Now she had no direction in her life. I tried to comfort her and we talked through some ideas, but I know she felt pretty worthless at that moment.]

NOVEMBER 2, 2023

Lord, here I am again just waiting . . . waiting . . . waiting, trying to not grow weary as I see her doing not much but binge-watching her shows and binge-eating—I'm so afraid she is going to go back to purging again. Lord, ultimately You know just what it will take for her to come back to You, and so I pray once again that You give her what she needs—although that prayer nearly destroyed me this year. [If I only knew what a profound prayer this was and what it would soon mean for us all.] But please keep holding me and Steve up (and holding us together) while You do the work in her. And Lord, please provide, as only You can, to help pay for all her medical bills, therapy, and more. [God answered even this prayer, although again not how I would have planned or wanted. Friends and family came through in the biggest way with meals and financial help, so much so that it paid off almost all of what we had drained over the years of her treatments.] I feel as if I'm constantly sinking—help me keep my eyes fixed on You in this storm.

NOVEMBER 6, 2023

Give me only what will serve You best, and may it be used to reveal the greatest of all Your mercies; bringing glory to Your name through me, according to Your will (quoted in Cowman 418). Then I followed up with a note: There is no reason for pain except for our good and His glory.

[If only I had known that one week later this very prayer that I underlined and highlighted would be fulfilled. I always thought it would be some huge life transformation in Minnie that all the world would see, but instead it was the Lord taking her home, and what the world would be looking at was me! Is this what Jesus meant when He said, "Unless a kernel of wheat falls to the ground and dies, it remains only a single seed. But if it dies, it produces many seeds" (John 12:24 NIV)? Just like God, this was the verse in my devotional on what began as a normal Tuesday, November 14. I read this in the morning, and then went about my day with appointments around town, not knowing my precious baby's body lay lifeless in the next room. I would not find her until mid-day, when I finally came home and went in to check on her.]

NOVEMBER 14, 2023, AND THE DAYS LEADING UP TO IT

Minnie had been going out every evening with friends. One particular evening, she called me and was clearly shaken. She had just seen *him,* and he saw her and made it known that he saw her. She was almost in tears when she called and she kept saying, "I'm not okay." Steve immediately said that it's going to mess her up. We had no idea of how badly she would be affected.

Sunday night (November 12): Minnie said she was hanging out

with a friend, but since we did not trust her, we would often check her location. We saw that she drove to Los Angeles, stopped briefly at a fast food place, then turned around and came home. While she was gone, Steve was looking for something and I told him to check Minnie's room. He came out with weed pens he had found in her drawer. She was at it again. When she came home she announced that she and her friend had taken a joyride to LA for fun; she knew we were watching. We confronted her about the weed, and she was forthcoming but also said she just could not sleep and needed it. We talked about some solutions and I told her we could figure out a way to get her the help she needed. Later that night she came out with her trash can full of all her junk and made a big show of throwing it all away, trying to convince us that she was done with all of it. When I walked into her room to say good night, I noticed a smell like burnt plastic. I told her she looked pale. She jumped up and said, "I feel fine!" I immediately had suspicion, and I asked her about it. Later I googled "drugs with plastic smell when burnt" and several came up, including Percocet. I guess I put it out of my mind because I did not think she would do that, although I think a part of me knew. I have replayed these couple of days repeatedly, wishing I would have confronted her more aggressively. Then again, had I done that, she probably would have run out, taken her stuff with her, and someone would have found her body on the street somewhere. She was going to do what she was going to do, so as painful as it is, I guess I am thankful it was at home.

Monday (November 13): She got up late and said she felt sick, nauseated. I told her to just lay low, and I kept a close watch on her. I smelled the burning plastic again, and once again I asked her about it; nothing. Later in the day she made a show of telling me she now smelled it too, so "together" we tried to find the source. That evening she still wasn't feeling good—I now know it was from the Percocet she was taking, so I just went into her room before I went to bed and I told her I loved her. . . . That was the last time I saw my precious baby alive.

Tuesday, November 14, began like all the other days, except something woke me up around 4:30 a.m.; I am convinced that this is when she took her last breath and my mommy connection knew it in my spirit. She had sent Francesca a Snapchat around 4:00 a.m. (6:00 a.m. Francesca's time), and Francesca replied—but Minnie never responded. I'm sure it was at that time Minnie would be burning and inhaling what she *thought* was another Percocet, but instead it was fentanyl: the mistake that would take her life and change mine forever.

NOVEMBER 15, 2023

This is the day after You took my beautiful Minnie from me. How do I even put words on a page? God, I have so many unanswered prayers. The last three years have been an unbearable struggle—for me and for Minnie. She was so tortured by mental health and demonic power so strong—all she wanted to do was numb her pain. But just as it seemed she was moving in the right direction . . . this! I question what I thought I knew about You and Your promises.

> *Each one of us felt the burden of grief followed by the freedom of peace in its place falling over us.*

[Family and friends gathered around us to try to bring comfort, and in many ways they did. The prayers that were prayed for us and over us were felt so powerfully. They held us up with the power of the Holy Spirit in ways I cannot put into words. A cherished group of friends went immediately to work on getting Francesca to me, and when they dropped her off first thing in the morning, my heart knew I could hold on. The next to show up was Steve's sister from Texas. She brings the fragrance of Christ with her wherever she goes, and even nonbelievers feel it. I felt His comfort arrive with her that day. Later, my entire family came over, and somehow we all congregated in Minnie's room after a precious friend had come and cleaned up wreckage left by Minnie's passing. That was truly an act of selfless love! As we all gathered and talked and sat in disbelief, my daddy prayed—oh, how he prayed! He prayed that the demonic stronghold over that room would be broken and that the Lord would redeem and restore the years that the devouring locust had stolen (Joel 2:25). It was a significant and unforgettable time, and it brought our family together with a bond that no one else could ever understand. Each one of us felt the burden of grief followed by the freedom of peace in its place falling over us. After they all left, Francesca, Steve, and I sat up all night and looked at pictures and just talked about so many memories. We laughed, we cried, we reminisced; but really, we were hurting, questioning God, questioning if Minnie was in heaven. We needed Him more than ever. We needed Him to speak.

5

THE PROMISE

C. H. Von Bogatzky wrote, "He [God] generally waits to send His help until the time of our greatest need, so that His hand will be plainly seen in our deliverance. He chooses this method so we will not trust anything that we may see or feel, as we are so prone to do, but will place our trust solely on His Word" (quoted in Cowman 423). When we *hear from God* we must test it against the Scripture. Did God say it? Is it a promise that has already been recorded? All Scripture is there for us, even today. Yes, it was written over a span of thousands of years, but there is nothing in the Bible that I cannot claim for *me*. That being said, I want to revisit with you the promise God gave me from Psalm 27:13. As I mentioned before, when He gave me that promise, I asked Him to constantly remind me of the promise by sending me butterflies because Minnie loved butterflies (as they signify emerg-

"Where is my butterfly story?"

ing beauty out of a struggle). I can say in all honesty that in the year leading up to her death I have never seen more butterflies, circling all around my yard and even in odd places like the freeway! And it seemed that during those darkest moments He would always send the biggest, most beautiful ones across my path. God was constantly reminding me. The day before Minnie's death, I was in the kitchen for hours, and right outside the window were fluttering butterflies all day long. I told myself, *God must be working in her life! And He is reminding me that He is doing something amazing. I can't wait!*

When I found my precious Minnie, I immediately and helplessly began chest compressions in an attempt to resuscitate her. I knew it was futile, and as I kept trying in vain, I shouted to God, "This wasn't the promise!" I had put all my hope, all my trust in Him, and at that moment it seemed He had failed me. I could not believe that this God I based my entire life upon had let me down. It could not be! I knew what He promised, I knew who He was, and I knew He would never let me down.

Isaiah 7:11 says, "Ask the Lord your God for a sign, whether in the deepest depths or in the highest heights" (NIV).

The morning after Minnie passed, my sweet niece texted the family that she had had a dream. "I dreamt that I was walking into heaven and I saw her, and she was happier than ever. . . . God is giving me this sense of overwhelming peace that she is with Him." I had forgotten to turn off my phone alarm that morning, and while I was reading her text, the alarm went off (which was actually the same ringtone I had set for Minnie), the song "Whom the Son Sets Free Is Free Indeed" (Hillsong 2019). Was this God speaking to me? Was He confirming that she was truly saved and was with Him? The next day another family member had a dream about her, and in the dream Minnie was happy and whole. *God, why are You talking to everyone but me? I am the one who needs to know she is with You. Why are You not giving* me *dreams about her?*

NOVEMBER 16, 2023

Lord, I question if those promises I thought I heard from You were real. Everyone is telling me she's with You, free from pain and suffering, skin perfect and healed, mind free from torment—oh, how I want to believe it, how I need to *know* it! That's been my only prayer, that's my only prayer now, but I feel as if my prayers are hitting the ceiling. The grief, the anguish, the pain is just too much—yet that's what my girl fought every single day of her short life. She struggled with the truth we taught her from birth because of the torment from the demonic strongholds over her. She longed to be free, so she numbed the pain. Was taking her Your way of saving her? Why are You silent, God? I need to hear You, I need You to wipe away my horrible memories from when I found her, and I need You to tell me loud and clear that You are holding my Minnie in Your arms that I had always prayed she would run to. I will never have peace until You give me that assurance that You held true to Your promises to me—all the promises I've written down over the last several years, promises I've claimed daily . . . because if Your promises are not true, then what *do* I believe in? And if they're not true, then my own salvation isn't real—so they *must* be true!

[Once I could think clearly and took my thoughts captive in obedience to Him (2 Corinthians 10:5), I realized that He truly did show me His goodness. When the psalmist wrote in Psalm 34:18, "The Lord is close to the brokenhearted and saves those who are crushed in spirit" (NIV), the Lord knew that verse would one day be for me. Let me tell you the most beautiful story of how I truly learned just how merciful, loving, and gracious God is and how much He really does care about His children.]

NOVEMBER 27, 2023

Where do I even begin? Let me begin with praise and thanksgiving because of Your great love, mercy, and faithfulness. On the 17th

I finally got out of the house. I had not left the house for a few days. Finally my neighbor said she wanted to do something for me, and since she is my hairdresser, her love language was to wash my hair to show me some love. Since it was a pretty day, I decided to walk to her house. When I was done, I stepped onto the sidewalk and looked up at the beautiful blue sky and I said out loud, "Lord, I need to know Minnie is with You—send me a butterfly," and at the very moment those words left my mouth, a huge yellow butterfly flew right across my path! Remember: this was the middle of November—definitely *not* butterfly season! I nearly collapsed on the street and ran home sobbing to tell Steve. Later, my dear friends came over to visit me, and I told them about the amazing miracle. Then we went into Minnie's room to talk, and one friend exclaimed, "A yellow butterfly!" I had forgotten that I had found a little plastic yellow butterfly in Minnie's drawer a few days prior, and I had put it on her nightstand. Lord, You confirmed Your confirmation!

The next day, my other daughter and her friend went to breakfast and she told her friend about the butterfly story. They were looking for parking, and my daughter said her friend passed up many spots, and as she turned down an alley to park, my daughter sadly sighed, "Where is *my* butterfly story?" As they turned down the alley, there it was—a huge butterfly painted on the wall, and they had never seen it there before! Later that day my husband went to get his hair cut, and his usual hairdresser was not there, so they assigned him a different lady he had never seen before—and she had butterfly tattoos all the way down her arm. God was speaking to each of us in a way we could all understand.

But just like God, He didn't stop there. I decided to go through our drawer with old cards we had given each other over the years, but what I found was a treasure I cannot even put into words. There was Minnie's journal she had written when she was eight years old. I don't remember it, but I had written a date on it at some point. As I flipped through the pages of her little drawings and things, I came upon the most amazing gift from the Lord—Minnie's own honest confession of faith written by her in her journal! Let me share with you her heart before the darkness attacked her.

> Awesome God—I cry in happy tears because of you and I'm so glad that you made me so I can love Jesus. You are my God and I will always be a Christian girl, and I will love you all my life. I will serve you all of my life. Jesus, you make me so happy. I just want my whole family to float up to heaven so we can go face to face with you.

And a second entry:

> Jesus, you are my holy God. You reign forever and you love us as we love you, but you love us even more than we can ever imagine. Lord, we are nothing compared to you. Jesus, you are mighty and wonderful. You are great and powerful. Jesus, you died on the cross for our sins because you love us. You are so big and we are so small compared to you. You are more than love. You are breaking our sins apart. Lord, I don't know what I would do without you. I love you with my whole heart. I am sooooooo glad I asked you into my heart. I am so happy that I am a Christian. You are the best thing that I can think about. *For God so loved the world that He gave His only begotten Son, that whosoever would believe in Him would not perish but have everlasting life* (John 3:16). God, you are bigger than anything.

Wow—wow—wow! God had been using my pastor to speak the truth into my life that you cannot lose your salvation; there is nothing you can do to lose it because there is nothing you can do to earn it in the first place. Jesus did it all, and once we are His, nothing can pluck us from His hand—and Minnie *believed* and *confessed*, so at that moment, God assured me that she was with Him! No more pain, no more torment, no more lies, no more temptations, no more medications and drugs to try to get through life, no more nightmares, no more sin; just my baby in the loving, merciful, and faithful arms of her Savior. Many times since then, God has solidified this message in my heart over and over through other Bible teachers I learn from. As the song by Big Daddy Weave (2023) says, *Heaven changes everything.*

Another way He showed me His lovingkindness was through a song I just heard on the radio for the first time, TobyMac's "Faithfully." How was it that this song was written just for me? I remembered a few years back hearing that TobyMac's son had passed away, so I dug a little more deeply into the story. What I found was both tragic and solace to me. His son had died just like my Minnie, by an accidental fentanyl poisoning from trying to numb the pain of mental illness with drugs. He thought he was purchasing an opioid but it was laced with fentanyl, and he was found dead. The words of this song came alive to me and have encouraged and reassured me in those darkest hours that I will make it. 2 Corinthians 1:3–5 says, "Blessed be the God and Father of our Lord Jesus Christ, the Father of mercies and God of all comfort, who comforts us in all our tribulation, that we may be able to comfort those who are in any trouble, with the comfort with which we ourselves are comforted by God." The Lord provided TobyMac the comfort he needed, inspired him to write "Faithfully," and that became the comfort I have desperately needed to help sustain me. I don't believe it was a coincidence that this song was just released on the radio. The Lord works out every detail of our lives if we love and trust Him.

NOVEMBER 27, 2023 (CONTINUED)

O Lord, these two weeks have been unreal, so indescribably hard, so filled with tears and sadness . . . *but God!* The way You have brought us peace that truly passes understanding, the way You have brought an army of friends and family around us to lift us up and strengthen us—and I know You're not done working! Looking back through my prayers, I came to December 8, 2021—I prayed that not only would You bring Minnie to repentance like the prodigal son but that also You would use her life for the salvation of many people I named specifically, just as with Joseph when he told his brothers "What you meant for evil God meant for good and for the salvation of many." That has been my prayer all these years—that You would use Minnie's struggles and her life for the salvation of many—and that was always her desire as well, to help others.

Well, all of those I've been praying for have heard the truth of Your Word, both at the funeral and just being here with us during this horrible time of grief. You've opened my mouth in boldness, and I know Your Word does not return void. You have already accomplished the salvation of Minnie for Your glory, so Lord, now I am pleading with You in full confidence that I will see the salvation of many, which You promised. If her death means eternal life for all my loved ones, then I accept it as a gift from You! Lord, You saved my Minnie! You know she had too many demons, too much guilt, too many secrets, too much pain—and You saved her! I know someday I will see how You fit all the pieces together, as I knew You were doing, but for now I will rest, knowing my girl is finally safe and healed and whole. It will be strange for me not needing to pray for her anymore, as it was all-consuming for years, but I know I have the rest of my family members, who need Your comfort, help, and strength, so they are now my priority in prayer, along with my unsaved loved ones.

Lord, thank You.

[If you know God, you know that when He makes a point, He makes it for all to see! I am still waiting to see all the souls who will be saved because of her death, although I am aware that I may never know until I get to heaven. If nothing else, I want others to see what a life of true faith and total dependence upon God looks like in the face of the raging storm. I want them to remember how the Lord has been my help when they, in turn, go through various trials. I want them to ask me about the hope that I have so I can tell them about my Jesus (1 Peter 3:15).]

Lord, I want to see many souls saved; I need her death to mean something!

6

THE REMINDER

Shortly after we buried our beautiful girl, a dear friend came to visit with something special she wanted to give me. Minnie had spent a lot of special time with her recently, and one of those times was a trip to a vintage shop, where she bought Minnie some unique items, including a perfect red dress we would end up burying her in. This same friend went back to the store to find a piece for herself after Minnie passed, something special to remind her of Minnie. She told the owners (a mother and son) what happened, and they all cried together. Then she told them why she was there. The son told her he had *just* the right thing. When they were shopping together a few weeks prior, Minnie was looking at the jewelry case in back, and she picked up a beautiful antique pin. She had told the son she loved it so much and

> *The more time goes by, I am more and more convinced that God had to take Minnie to rescue her.*

wanted it, but it was too expensive. He went back to the case, and it was still there, so he brought it to my friend. Can you guess what it was? A stunning yellow butterfly pin! God had already been setting the stage for the yellow butterfly, even before it became my story. That is our amazing, timeless God!

As I write this, I am continuing to work through the phases of grief, and I have been in a time of questioning God once again—maybe not questioning as much as it is wondering. As I shared, He has shown His incredible mercies to me to help calm my fears. He has given me miraculous signs over and over in the days and weeks following Minnie's *relocation*. (I started using this term instead of *death* because I realized that she was very much alive—just in a different location!) He has *quieted me with His love* (Zephaniah 3:17) and comforted me with His goodness. But I will confess that I have been once again questioning how it could be true that Minnie is with Him. Was her conversion as a child real? Did she cry out to Jesus as she was taking her last breath? I've been begging God for yet another sign to remind me, but He has been seemingly silent.

In my Bible reading the other day He brought me to the story of when He called Moses to lead the Israelites out of Egypt (Exodus 3–12). Moses made every excuse for why he could not do it and he questioned God with each answer from the Almighty. The Lord even told Moses His precious name "I AM," and still Moses questioned. Finally God's anger burned against Moses, and then it hit me that I am no longer like Gideon asking for a sign, but I am like Moses, who got the signs and yet still questioned. Since that time I realize that, as with Moses, the Lord not only gave me the signs but also has revealed to me who He is. All the Scriptures tell of His character. Let me reiterate Psalm 103:2–18 (NLT) again, because it deserves another look:

> May I never forget the good things he does for me.
> He forgives all my sins
>   and heals all my diseases.

He redeems me from death
   and crowns me with love and tender mercies.
He fills my life with good things.
   My youth is renewed like the eagle's!
The Lord gives righteousness
   and justice to all who are treated unfairly.
He revealed his character to Moses
   and his deeds to the people of Israel.
The Lord is compassionate and merciful,
   slow to get angry and filled with unfailing love.
He will not constantly accuse us,
   nor remain angry forever.
He does not punish us for all our sins;
   he does not deal harshly with us, as we deserve.
For his unfailing love toward those who fear him
   is as great as the height of the heavens above the earth.
He has removed our sins as far from us
   as the east is from the west.
The Lord is like a father to his children,
   tender and compassionate to those who fear him.
For he knows how weak we are;
   he remembers we are only dust.
Our days on earth are like grass;
   like wildflowers, we bloom and die.
The wind blows, and we are gone—
   as though we had never been here.
But the love of the Lord remains forever
   with those who fear him.
His salvation extends to the children's children
   of those who are faithful to his covenant,
   of those who obey his commandments!

DECEMBER 31, 2023

Lord, Your mercy, goodness, and faithfulness have blown me away once again. You know I've been really in a deep sadness this week, struggling to get through each day. You know I've been questioning what You showed me—the signs Minnie is with You. My mind wondered, Was her childhood confession of faith real? Did she know what it meant? Did You really save her when she had gone so far away? You know my heart and my questioning and praying for another sign. I took the dogs on a walk and I was praying. I looped around at my neighbor's house and said out loud, "Lord, please give me another sign." As I walked back past my neighbor's house (which I've passed on every single walk and even stopped to talk to him often), there in his garden was a yellow butterfly garden stake! I had never seen that before—what a gift! What a faithful God You are! As we close out this year of pain and sadness, I know that whatever 2024 brings is Jesus-filtered, and You will be with me every step of the way.

JANUARY 14, 2024

Lord, it's been two months, but even in my pain You're showing Your love and faithfulness. I woke up this morning with the song "Come, Jesus, Come" (McWhirter 2023) on repeat in my head—Your hope is my comfort, and You were reminding me of that hope, knowing I would have to face today (I was finally going to go back to church after two months, only because my son was asking me to take him). Then church—it's as though You planned the worship set just for me. I actually think You did! "See a Victory" (Elevation Worship 2020) was first; the part about "You take what the enemy meant for evil, and You turn it for good"—yes! You were speaking loud and clear to me through my tear-stained cheeks. Then they sang a song I have never heard them sing in all the time we've been going there, "It Is Well" (Bethel Music 2014), the very same one we had sung at the funeral! Again, You were speaking directly to me in all my pain. (Later when I told Francesca about it, she said they sang the same exact song at her church in Texas, and she also had never heard them sing that song! Wow!) I realize more and more each day that it was because of Your great love for Minnie that You had to take her home. I also realize that it was my great love for her that made me hold onto her so tightly—but also it was because of that same great love for her that I eventually had to release her into Your hands, the hardest prayer I ever prayed. Lord, I know You were the fourth man in the fire this whole time, and I know You will continue being there and showing Yourself so real, so near, so faithful, so good, so merciful, and so loving. Come quickly, Lord!

JANUARY 17, 2024

> *God has never failed me. Even in my greatest difficulties, heaviest trials, and deepest poverty and need, He has never failed me. Because I was enabled by God's grace to trust Him, He has always come to my aid* (quoted in Cowman 35, 37). "One day I came to know Dr. John Douglas Adam," wrote Charles Gallaudet Trumbull. "I learned he considered his greatest spiritual asset to be his unwavering awareness of the actual presence of Jesus. Nothing sustained him as much, he said, as the realization that Jesus was always actually present with him. This realization was totally independent of his own feelings, his worthiness, and his perceptions as to how Jesus would demonstrate His presence" (quoted in Cowman 37).

[You will see as you keep reading through my personal testimony just how real Jesus has been, just how near He has been, and how He has never failed me in spite of what happed to my Minnie. If not for His presence, I could not take another breath. If not for the fact that He lives, I could not face tomorrow.]

FAITH IN ACTION:

REMEMBERING WHAT GOD HAS DONE

Remember His marvelous works which He has done,
His wonders, and the judgments of His mouth
(Psalm 105:5).

I will remember the works of the Lord;
surely I will remember Your wonders of old. I
will also meditate on all Your work, and talk of Your deeds
(Psalm 77:11–12).

And you shall remember that the Lord your God led you
(Deuteronomy 8:2).

JANUARY 18, 2024

"Thanks be to God, who always leads us in triumph in Christ" (2 Corinthians 2:14.) God wins His greatest victories through apparent defeats. . . . But then He comes in and upsets the work of the enemy, overthrows the apparent victory, and as the Bible says, "frustrates the ways of the wicked" (Psalm 146:9 NIV). Consequently, He gives us a much greater victory than we would have known had He not allowed the enemy seemingly to triumph in the first place. . . . "For no other god can save in this way" (Daniel 3:29 NIV). . . . May we learn

that in all the difficult places God takes us, He is giving us opportunities to exercise our faith in Him that will bring about blessed results and greatly glorify His name (quoted in Cowman 37, 38).

FEBRUARY 7, 2024

Our hope will not be in vain, and in the Lord's own timing help will come. . . . When it seemed impossible for help to come, it did come, for God has His own unlimited resources. In ten thousand different ways, and at ten thousand different times, God's help may come to us (quoted in Cowman 65).

[The more time goes by, I am more and more convinced, as I've said before, that God had to take Minnie to rescue her. Obviously He could have done it in ten thousand other, different ways, but He did the impossible when He rescued her. The help I always prayed for finally came—His ultimate salvation.]

MARCH 12, 2024

Lord, You know today I have been praying and crying out to You asking for reassurance that Minnie is with You. Going back and reading my journal makes me embarrassed and remorseful that I waivered so much, even after the Lord had shown me His goodness time after time. Like the man who asked Jesus to heal his son, I pray, "Lord, I believe; help my unbelief" (Mark 9:24). I sat down to study Your Word, and as always, I started by reading Streams in the Desert. *In today's reading was a quote from Mark Guy Pearse, and I knew it was You immediately and directly answering me yet again: "Today, only questions surround your great sorrow, but then you will see how the threatening enemy was actually swept away during your stormy night of fear and grief. Today you see only your loss, but then you will see how God used it to break the evil chains that had begun to restrain you. Today you cower at the howling wind and the roaring thunder, but then you will see how they beat back the waves of destruction and opened your way to the peaceful Land of Promise"* (quoted in Cowman 111).

[This was as if God was telling me, as I've known and said before, that He used the storm for His purpose, to bring my Minnie to His ultimate peace. Thank You, Lord, for listening, for hearing, and for loving me enough to speak to me like this! Thank You for being so patient and kind as You teach me more of Your truth.]

Friend, you are on this journey with me, and I hope you can feel my heart as God has been working in me. Over and over I had the conversation with God about *How could she possibly be in heaven when she was in such a dark place?*

Then just the other day a friend sent me a podcast by my pastor, and it was again like God directly answering my prayer. For all of you praying parents who might have a child who once gave his or her life to Jesus and has since turned away, you would do well to listen to the podcast "Will Backsliders

If you're discouraged or doubting, keep your ship anchored to the only Rock, and He will never let you sink.

Be Raptured?" (Hibbs 2024). Although different than the rapture, it truly was an answer from God, once and for all setting my heart and mind at peace. My pastor used the scripture of 1 Corinthians 5:1–5, and I never quite understood it until now. There was someone in the church who was living in overt sin, and Paul told the church, "Deliver such a one to Satan for the destruction of the flesh, that his spirit may be saved in the day of the Lord Jesus." I finally understand that this means sometimes God needs to let Satan physically destroy a backslidden Christian (thinking he won), but truly that is God's way of saving that person from destruction so the person's soul can finally be free from the sin he or she was entangled in. The natural consequence for Minnie's sin was physical death, but God used it to free her soul from the earthly torment she could not escape. Her death was God's mercy for her soul and truly mercy for her earthly agony. Jesus came thundering into Minnie's room that early morning on a rescue mission, and He pulled her out of her bondage with one powerful, merciful move of His hand.

As the lyrics of the song "He Brought Me Back to Life" (Bethel 2021) say, "The enemy thought he had me, but Jesus said, 'You are mine.'" And as she got her first glimpse of heaven, I can only try to fathom how she jumped and shouted, "Hell lost another one—now I am free!" (Maverick City Music et al. 2021). You can see how worship music has played a vital role in my life, my struggles, and my healing.

Minnie loved music too, and if she could have a theme song in heaven, I'm sure it would be "Greater Still" (Brandon Lake 2022). I can picture my girl singing this with all her heart, face to face with her Savior.

I can be confident that He faithfully completed the good work He began in Minnie so many years ago, just as He said He would in Philippians 1:6. I realize that Jesus has been tenderly showing me His love to carry me through, but what He truly wants from me is complete trust in Him, in which He does not need to keep showing me those signs because my faith is steadfast and unwavering. James 1:6–8 tells us, "He who doubts is like a wave of the sea driven and tossed by the wind. For let not that man suppose that he will receive anything from the Lord; he is a double-minded man, unstable in all his ways." I have felt tossed back and forth over these last few years, but Jesus told us, "Blessed are those who have not seen and yet have believed" (John 20:29). I *do* believe, but I am thankful for His loving and gracious signs He has given my hurting heart.

Just today (only four months following Minnie's relocation), I was listening to the most beautiful testimony by Pastor Billy Crone and how the Lord saved him from a life of drugs, occultism, new age, and even demon possession. As amazing as his story was, it actually made me sad and question why God saved him out of a life so abhorrent and vile, yet He chose to take Minnie out of this world instead. I prayed as I took a long walk, asking the Lord for a word from His heart to mine.

When I got home I spoke to my dear friend Ro on the phone, and she could not wait to tell me a story. We have a gal (I'll call her Vee) who dog sits for us when we go out of town, and we were supposed to be leaving for our annual Thanksgiving trip just three days after Minnie's passing. I remember Vee texted me the morning of November 14 (the day my life turned upside down), checking to make sure we were still good to have her come house sit. At the time I still had not found Minnie, so I told her yes, we were all set.

Flash forward four months to today, and Vee and Ro were out to eat, and they were talking about Minnie and our family. Vee told Ro that the reason she texted me that morning was to check on me because she had a dream that night (the night Minnie died). She dreamt that Steve and I were at a cemetery standing over a casket but there were butterflies flying all around us, and it was tragic and beautiful. Let me reiterate—this is the night Minnie died! God would not send me the first butterfly confirmation for another several days. Then Ro told her the story about *my* butterfly confirmation a few days following Minnie's passing. Vee was absolutely shocked and told Ro that in her dream all the butterflies were yellow!

These amazing confirmations from the Lord are only just a few of these stories. I could go on and on, like the time when we were driving to Minnie's burial and there was a car in front of us on the freeway with butterfly stickers on the back. And then there was a thank-you card my sister found in her huge storage container. She has it piled high with various boxes from her entire adult life. She randomly opened a box, and there at the very top was a card with a big yellow butterfly; it was a thank-you card from Minnie, written when she was very young.

Oh, He is so good; He is so near to the brokenhearted! If you seek Him, you will find Him, and you will hear His voice.

I hope you are not tiring of my God confirmations, because as I write, He continues sending them. And as much as I would like to think I'm strong, or as I tell others, "I'm doing as good as I can be doing," really I am a broken and fragile soul beaten down by this life, and I desperately need God to keep whispering in my ear, or sometimes shouting at me that He's got her! And He's got *me*!

The reason I'm telling you these stories is to reinforce over and over that if you "draw near to God, He will draw near to you" (James 4:8) and that He really is right there if we only seek Him. He has shown time and time again that He really is "near to the brokenhearted."

Friend, if you're discouraged or doubting, keep your ship anchored to the only Rock and He will never let you sink. Yes, I go through periods where I just need that extra reassurance (call it female hormones or just waves of grief), but at the end of the day I remember all His promises and have claimed them for my own!

7

HIS GOODNESS IS RUNNING AFTER ME

So here I am yet again, nearly five months after Minnie left this earth, and God gave me two "big hugs" this week, just when I was physically and emotionally broken. First of all, I was mindlessly scrolling through Instagram one night and I saw my dog groomer had posted a picture of an adorable dog with the caption "Guess how old Minnie is turning." The caption caught my attention, of course, so I zoomed in on the picture and saw that Minnie was wearing a yellow butterfly bandana! Coincidence? God doesn't do coincidence. God does purposeful signs. Do you know that there is no equivalent of the word *coincidence* in the Hebrew language?

I don't want to make a career out of my pain.

The next day I went in Minnie's room to put something away, and a flash of yellow caught my eye. It was a book I used to read to her when she was a baby, titled *How Do I Kiss You?* (Weimer 2008), and I had put her baby picture in it, so when I would read it to her she would get a thrill. I had propped that book in her room on her bookshelf but somehow never noticed until that moment that the cover is actually a big yellow butterfly! Think about that! Eighteen years ago God was already setting in motion the signs He would use for this season of my life, knowing full well how I would so desperately need them. All of these years, yellow butterflies held zero significance to me, but God knew! This one really blew me away at how powerful the meaning was. Let's just say it was an ugly cry.

Flash forward to just yesterday while I was working around the house with worship music on, and the song "It Is Well" (Bethel 2014) came on, and God gently nudged me and said, "Remember when I did that for you?" Why are we so quick to forget His amazing and miraculous blessings?

That is why over and over in the Old Testament, Moses, the prophets, and the psalmists counseled the people to never stop talking about God's incredible miracles. He told them to build altars to remember where significant occurrences took place. Why? Because God knows how quickly we forget, and He also knows we need those constant reminders of how He has intervened in our lives. Perhaps that is why I've recorded all of these miraculous events here for you—to remind *me* during those times when I forget all the good He has shown me in the midst of the storm.

And I know that God will continue revealing His perfect plan to me—if not in this life, then when I stand before His throne. As Arthur Christopher Bacon so beautifully said, "I still believe that a day of understanding will come for each of us, however far away it may be. We will understand as we see the tragedies that today darken and dampen the presence of heaven for us take their proper place in God's great plan—a plan so overwhelming, magnificent, and joyful, we will laugh with wonder and delight" (quoted in Cowman 72).

In the end, I do not want to be remembered as someone who lost her daughter or as someone who suffered greatly. I don't want to make a career out of my pain. Instead, I want to be remembered as someone with whom the Lord walked through the fire and came out as pure gold, reflecting the image of Jesus. I want hope to be my anthem so that no one remembers the suffering, but instead, they see a life full of joy, even to my last breath.

8

HOPE AGAINST ALL HOPE

Following Minnie's relocation, many friends reached out with special words of encouragement, meaningful gifts, and books to help me through my journey. Two of these books, besides the Word of God, have been like a lifeline to me.

The first one that showed up on my doorstep was *Hope for Hurting Hearts,* by Pastor Greg Laurie. He wrote this book from a point of deep loss and anguish following the death of his son, so it was easy for me to identify with the raw emotions he put into print. He wrote about the story of Jesus raising Lazarus from the dead in John 11. I read and reread this passage, realizing *I* was acting like Martha when she said to Jesus, "Lord, if You had been here, my brother would not have died." But what Pastor Laurie stated, and what helped change my thinking, was "because Jesus wanted to do more than they were expecting" (Laurie 21). He goes on to quote Pastor Chuck Smith: "Never trade what you don't know for what you do know" (quoted in Laurie 27). I had to ask myself what it is I absolutely knew in spite of the fact that I had no idea, and still don't, what Jesus was doing.

I know that God loves Minnie
I know that God loves Me
I know that His thoughts toward me are for good and not harm (Jeremiah 29:11)
I know that although God is just, He is also merciful
I know that once you call on Jesus as Lord, you are sealed with the Holy Spirit for eternity
I know that Minnie called on Jesus as Lord as a young girl
I know there is nothing you can do to earn salvation, so there is nothing you can do to "un-earn" salvation
I know that God promised to give beauty for ashes, so
I know that God will bring good out of even this
I know I will see my Minnie again

Going forward with my new confidence that Minnie was with Jesus, I wanted to learn everything I could about heaven, as Pastor Laurie suggested. Was she floating around playing a harp? Standing in a sea of people just singing for eternity? Or was she experiencing something else, something far beyond anything that my mind could imagine? I grabbed every book about heaven that I could find, making sure they lined up with the Bible, and what I discovered not only gave me the most incredible picture of what Minnie was experiencing, but it also gave me such an intense and consuming longing to be there! Knowing that what awaits those of us who call upon Jesus is something so phenomenal, I am "righteously jealous" that my Minnie is already there but also beyond thankful that she is already there. As Pastor Laurie stated, "Heaven is what is real, earth is what is temporary. That is why C. S. Lewis described life on earth as 'the shadowlands.' Earth is only a pale version of heaven. Not the other way around" (Laurie 96). He goes on to say, "Think of the purest, highest, most ecstatic joy on earth, multiply it a thousand times, and you get a fleeting glimpse of heaven's euphoria" (Laurie 98).

One huge question I had was if Minnie knew what was going on down here, if she knew I missed her. Pastor Laurie said something so profound regarding this, and every time I think about it, my heart nearly erupts in my chest. He mentioned a scripture I've read several times, yet I always misunderstood it until he explained it thoroughly. It is Hebrews 12, which says, "Therefore we also, since we are surrounded by so great a cloud of witnesses, let us lay aside every weight, and the sin which so easily ensnares us, and let us run with endurance the race that is set before us." I always thought the "great cloud of witnesses" was those around us here on earth, but as my pastor always says, "We have to find out what the *therefore* is there for." Pastor Laurie said we need to look back at Hebrews 11 to see to whom this is referring. He states, "So who are the witnesses? One interpretation of this passage names them simply as people of faith who have gone before us . . . actually observing us and taking note of our progress in the faith. They are the cloud of witnesses watching us, and cheering us on" (Laurie 105).

With the strength of Jesus in me and with Minnie cheering me on, I can make it to the finish line!

Whoa! So my Minnie, whom I encouraged and cheered on for her eighteen years on earth, is now in heaven watching me and cheering me on to my finish line! Every time I want to break down and cave in, I think of my girl saying, "Come on, Mommy! You can do it! There's more work Jesus needs to do through you." It's like the lyrics to the song "Almost Home," by MercyMe: "Find strength in each step knowing heaven is cheering you on." I can make it! With the strength of Jesus in me and with Minnie cheering me on, I can make it to the finish line!

That is when the next book showed up on my doorstep and moved profoundly on my heart. The father-in-law of an old high school friend wrote *Hope When Your Heart Is Breaking* after the sudden loss of his dear wife. He penned a personal note to me inside the cover: "For in my time of greatest loss I was met by Jesus, bringing living hope to my broken heart. It is hope stronger than the storm and longer than the valley. He can go to places in your heart where no one else can go and do things no one else can do." He called this "defiant hope" and explained it this way:

> For hope to overcome despair in life's dark valleys, it has to be something more than the syrupy, unanchored variety usually offered to us. More than the Wikipedia definition of hope as "an optimistic attitude of mind, based on expectation of positive outcomes."
>
> This hope needs to be as real as the hurt. As strong as the grief. As compelling as the fear. As powerful as the pull to give up. . . .
>
> I've seen hope that failed to deliver, like a light that goes out when you're in the dark. But I've also seen the kind of hope that keeps lighting up the darkness. Defiant hope. Hope that finds the healing presence of God Himself in the midst of the rubble. A hope that shakes its fist at despair and fear and shouts, "No! You can't have me!" (Hutchcraft 16).

Summed up, *hope is a choice*! "So there's a decision to be made. To challenge hopelessness. To resist. Not to deny the pain, but to refuse to be defined by the pain. . . . Hope is a fist in the face of surrender" (Hutchcraft 33). He continues:

> If we don't choose, grief will make us harder rather than softer. More angry rather than more at peace. More about "me" instead of more about others. More alone instead of more connected. More closed rather than more open. More hurting instead of healing. Hope is a choice. Not a feeling. Not a natural inclination. Not denial. A choice. It is a fist in the face of surrender. (Hutchcraft 81)

Hutchcraft's conclusion to the matter was "This hope is not a program, not a pill, not a religion or a belief. It's a *Person*" (Hutchcraft 37). Who is this Person?

9

DO YOU HAVE THIS HOPE?

First Thessalonians 4:13–14 says, "Brothers and sisters, we do not want you to be uninformed about those who sleep in death, so that you do not grieve like the rest of mankind, who have no hope. For we believe that Jesus died and rose again, and so we believe that God will bring with Jesus those who have fallen asleep in him" (NIV). Many have said to me, "I am so glad you have your faith," or "I don't know how you do it." Friends, it is *only* because of this hope I have in Jesus, the reassurance that I *will* see my Minnie again because of the gift of salvation. She is with Jesus and one day I will be there too. *This* is how I go on each day! And because of my hope, I want to bring that hope to others too. Yes, my soul is crushed by the weight of this grief, but I want others to see that this reassurance I have through Him gives me the strength to face each day. What good would I be to those around me if I sat in a crumpled pile of tears and brokenness every day? J. R. Miller spoke directly to me when he penned these words:

Yesterday you experienced a great sorrow, and now your home seems empty. Your first impulse is to give up and to sit down in despair amid your dashed hopes. Yet you must defy that temptation, for you are at the front line of the battle, and the crisis is at hand. Faltering even one moment would put God's interest at risk. Other lives will be harmed by your hesitation, and His work will suffer if you simply fold your hands. You must not linger at this point, even to indulge your grief. . . . Weeping inconsolably beside a grave will never bring back the treasure of a lost love, nor can any blessing come from such great sadness. Sorrow causes deep scars and indelibly writes its story on the suffering heart. We never completely recover from our greatest griefs and are never exactly the same after having passed through them. Yet sorrow that is endured in the right spirit impacts our growth favorably and brings us a greater sense of compassion for others. . . . Sitting down and brooding over our sorrow deepens the darkness surrounding us, allowing it to creep into our heart. And soon our strength has changed to weakness. But if we will turn from the gloom and remain faithful to the calling of God, the light will shine again and we will grow stronger. (quoted in Cowman 108, 109).

Job so beautifully articulated his hope in the Lord when, even in the midst of the worst unimaginable afflictions, he spoke the words "The Lord gave, and the Lord has taken away. Blessed be the name of the Lord" (Job 1:21), and later, "Though He slay me, yet will I trust Him" (Job 13:15).

Do you have this hope, this reassurance that our suffering is not for nothing, and the promise of an eternity with no tears, pain, loss, grief, and suffering?

The other day a friend sent me a lighthearted but accurate illustration of how to get to heaven:

> A man dies and goes to heaven. St. Peter meets him at the pearly gates and says, "Here's how it works. You need one hundred points to make it into heaven. You tell me all the good things you've done, and I give you a certain number of points for each item, depending on how good it was. When you reach one hundred points, you get in."
>
> "Okay," the man says. "I was married to the same woman for fifty years and never cheated on her, even in my heart."
>
> "That's wonderful," says St. Peter. "That's worth two points!"
>
> "Two points?" he says. "Well, I attended church all my life and supported its ministry with my tithe and service."
>
> "Terrific!" says St. Peter. "That's certainly worth a point."
>
> "One point? Well, I started a soup kitchen in my city and worked in a shelter for homeless veterans."
>
> "Fantastic—that's good for two more points," St.

Peter says.

"Two points?" Exasperated, the man cries, "At this rate the only way I'll get into heaven is by the grace of God!"

"Bingo!" St. Peter says. "One hundred points! Come on in!"

Now here is the point of this illustration. Many people try with all their earthly might to scrape and claw their way to God. But like this man, what people don't realize is that God has already made the way for us when He sent Jesus to pay our debt and make a way to Him through His death in our place. There is nothing, absolutely nothing we can do to earn our way to heaven. It is truly by the grace of God alone.

You've now read over and over in this book how some of the attributes of God are love, mercy, and grace. But what is grace? Let's look at it this way: God is the judge in a courtroom, and we have *all* broken His laws. (Romans 3:23 says, "All have sinned and fall short of the glory of God.") Unfortunately, the penalty for breaking even the least of God's laws is death (Genesis 3:3)—we all get the death penalty! However, our lawyer, our advocate

How could anyone turn down this unbelievable gift?

before the judge, is Jesus Himself, and He tells the judge that *He* will take the death penalty in our place. (Romans 6:23 says, "The wages of sin is death, but the gift of God is eternal life," and Romans 8:1: "There is therefore now no condemnation for those who are in Christ Jesus"). Now all we have to do is *accept* that gift by believing in Jesus and confessing that you accept His gift. Romans 10:9–10 states, "If you confess with your mouth the Lord Jesus and believe in your heart that God has raised Him from the dead, you will be saved. For with the heart one believes unto righteousness, and with the mouth confession is made unto salvation." And we read in Romans 10:13, "Whoever calls on the name of the Lord shall be saved." How could anyone turn down this unbelievable gift? We have been given an escape from the death penalty, but most people will not accept it, usually out of pride. Remember the man in the short story—he thought all his good works could get him into heaven. But our redemption is as easy as accepting His gift! For Jesus, it cost Him everything—but He did it out of *love*!

I heard a quote that speaks to this: "If we believe in Jesus we will die only once, but if we do not believe in Him we will die twice." Hebrews 9:27 says, "It is appointed for men to die once, but after this the judgment." There is no reincarnation; there are no second chances. The first death is the physical death we will all experience, but if we have accepted His gift of grace, we will live eternally with Him. However, if we do not accept that gift, there is a second death, a judgment, in which those who rejected Jesus will get *what they wanted*—eternity in hell away from Jesus, the second death. No one who goes to hell is ever *sent* there; if someone ends up in hell, he or she *chose* to go there. Today, while you still have breath in your lungs, I beg you to choose Jesus—choose life!

How do I choose Jesus?

Accept that you are a sinner in need of a Savior (you can't save yourself).

- Romans 3:10 says, "There is none righteous; no, not one."
- Romans 3:23 says, "All have sinned and fall short of the glory of God."

- Romans 6:23 says, "The wages of sin is death, but the gift of God is eternal life."

Believe in Jesus and who He is.

- Romans 10:9 says, "If you confess with your mouth the Lord Jesus and believe in your heart that God has raised Him from the dead, you will be saved."

Call on Jesus to forgive your sins and give you eternal life

- Romans 10:10, 13 tells us, "With the heart one believes unto righteousness, and with the mouth confession is made unto salvation . . . for whoever calls on the name of the Lord shall be saved."

Don't put off the most important decision of your life even a moment longer!

10

MY PLEA TO YOU FROM MY HEART

Let's talk about another decision that needs to be made before you take your last breath. As you can see, the last few years of my relationship with Minnie were very difficult, with so many highs and lows. Truth be told, there were many more low points than happy ones. On that last night of her life, my very last moment with her, in spite of a difficult day knowing she was hiding something from us, instead of going toe to toe with her, I just tucked her hair behind her ear and said, "I love you, Dolly." And those were the last words I ever spoke to her.

Why am I telling you this? My amazing daddy and mom (God bless loud, emotional Italians) have always had loud arguments. They would yell at each other and say stupid things, but then moments later they would be apologizing, kissing, and making up; they still do! They taught me such a valuable lesson in life—never go to bed angry at each other. Be the first to apologize. Make peace with those you love. Now, I cannot say I have always held fast to all these rules, but as much as depends on me, I always try to make peace with my loved ones at the end of each day. It requires a heavenly dose of humility, but once you can swallow that lump of pride in your throat, the peace of God washes over you as you do your part in maintaining unity.

My earnest plea to you is this: if you have any broken relationships, do your part to mend them while you still have time. Don't let your last words be spoken in anger, or worse, not spoken at all. Not much breaks my heart like hearing about family members who don't speak to each other anymore, and often, as more time goes by, both parties forget what their original argument was in the first place. No one knows when our last breath will be, so make the most of whatever time you and your loved one have left.

Unforgiveness is like drinking poison and expecting the other person to die.

Has your loved one wronged you in a way you feel you can never forgive? You don't have to do it on your own strength. Let the Lord's love work through you, and watch what He can do. I've not only had to forgive with the strength of the Lord, but praise God, I have also been forgiven so much by Him! *That* is my motivation for forgiveness—because He forgave me of sins that drove the nails into His hands and feet! Who am I to not forgive others?

Years ago I heard the following saying, and there are versions of it everywhere: *Unforgiveness is like drinking poison and expecting the other person to die.* Unforgiveness will hurt only you, so forgive, do your part to mend relationships, take that step toward your loved one—today is the day while you still have a chance. You might not have a close, trusting, intimate relationship with them again, but "If it is possible, as far as it depends on you, live at peace with everyone" (Romans 12:18 NIV).

You will never regret making the effort to restore a broken relationship. In the end, you would be hard pressed to find someone who said, "I wish I had never made peace with that person." Instead, how many times do we hear people say, "I regret that I never called him [her]," or "I regret that my last words were spoken in anger," or "I wish I had said, 'I'm sorry.'" Those regrets will follow you to your grave, so as far as it depends on you, make the step toward restoration.

She modeled Jesus to me, and I wanted to have Him in my heart too.

I never want to give the impression that I did everything right. Believe me—circulating in my mind day and night is *what could I have done differently*, but His grace is greater than all my own guilt and regrets! One thing I can say that we as parents *did* do right was raising our children in a church founded on the truth of the Bible. We intentionally switched churches to one with a strong children's ministry, knowing the power of a strong youth group in our own lives. However, that was not the end of what we fed our children. As the Bible instructs us over and over in the Old Testament (Deuteronomy 6:7–9; 11:19-20; Proverbs 22:6), our role as parents is to constantly model Jesus to our children, talk about Him, teach them about Him in all areas of their lives. He is to be another member of our families because it is Jesus alone who holds us together. And the best part about this is that there are promises of blessings if we obey Him in this.

The reason I stress this is that our biggest ministry as parents is first and foremost in our own homes. Children need to know *what* we believe, but more importantly *why* we believe it. Be ready to answer hard questions they may ask (with the guidance from the Holy Spirit), and if you believed blindly because your parents did, then it is time for you to dig deeper into the truth of His Word and know *why*. Tragically, today all the statistics are against children raised in church who go off to college and are given compelling "evidence" about why God doesn't exist, and they come home rejecting their faith. They never knew *why* they believed what they believed, so when the cares of life hit them, it strangles out the truths they learned as kids, as in the parable of the sower in Matthew 13.

Let's look again at Proverbs 22:6: "Train up a child in the way he should go, and when he is old he will not depart from it." Compare this to 2 Timothy 3:16–17: "All Scripture is God-breathed and is useful for teaching, rebuking, correcting and training in righteousness, so that the servant of God may be thoroughly equipped for every good work" (NIV). We teach our children the Scriptures as we model Christ for them, and this equips them for the rest of their lives. If they are instructed on how to put on the armor of God, they will be able to stand against all the spiritual forces in the heavenly realm and the "flaming arrows of the evil one" (see Ephesians 6:10–18). When children are young, teach them the way to be saved, and lead them to the cross of Christ! Of course, they won't understand what it all means at the moment.

When my mom led me to Jesus on our brown leather couch so many years ago, I had no idea what the weight of my sin meant, nor did I understand the depth of the cross of Christ and His great love for us. All I knew was that my mom's life had changed and her heart was softened, and I responded to *that*. She modeled Jesus to me, and I wanted to have Him in my heart too. It wouldn't be until my teenage years, those rebellious teenage years, when I started to really understand sin, forgiveness, and grace. My walk with Jesus has been high and low throughout my life, with times of living in the light of His glory, and with times of trying to hide from Him in shame. *But* what always kept me running back to the cross was that foundation my parents had laid for me when I was a child! The moment I gave my heart to Jesus long ago, I was sealed with the Holy Spirit for all eternity (Ephesians 4:30) and all my rebellion, my questioning, my hiding could never separate me from the love of Christ nor "unseal" me (Romans 8:38–39). In Bible times a king would use his signet ring to place his seal on something, meaning it could not be broken, like a branding iron on our soul announcing, "This one is mine!"

Minnie gave her heart to Jesus as a child. She was sealed for eternity at that moment. Life broke her, beat her down, caused her to waiver, question, and run; *but God* had announced over her, "This one is mine!" The Holy Spirit kept tugging on her heart (as He does so well), even in her rebellion, and her friends told me she had been talking about going back to church shortly before she left this earth. None of her bad decisions could undo what He had already done. Oh, the glory of the cross and His overwhelming grace and mercy! And this is exactly why I stress the importance of training up your children with Jesus. We as parents get one opportunity with our young children, so we need to do what the Lord instructed and allow His grace to fill in all those places where we fall short.

11

JESUS WAS THERE

Now that you have shared my intimate thoughts and prayers, experienced my visceral responses not only to my grief but also to my many miracles, received a glimpse of Minnie's life and struggles, and maybe have accepted some of my heartfelt pleas to you, I want to share one last profoundly significant reflection with you.

She could not outrun His love, she could not out-sin His mercy, and she could not outlast His goodness.

Minnie's service was led by our brother-in-law Pastor Randy Ensey. He knew of Minnie's deep and complex struggles, and he knew of Minnie's faith as a child. I want to share with you the memorable, sincere, and personal words he penned to honor Jesus through the life and homecoming of our Minnie.

When man was bruised and battered by sin and left for dead, God made Himself a body to dwell in and came to where man was. He came to the inn where the travelers refreshed themselves. He came to the cottage where the mother prayed. He came to the village where the children romped into the fields where the harvest was gathered. He came to the marriage feast and the funeral. He came to the crowded city and the soothing seashore. He came to the agony and the cross.

Show me where men are tempted of the devil and I'll show you Jesus there. Show me where men have cried out in the darkness and I'll show you Jesus there. Where man has suffered, Jesus suffered. Where man has wept, Jesus wept. Where man has toiled, Jesus toiled. Where man has died, Jesus died.

He bore our griefs and carried our sorrows and made His grave with the wicked in His death. He came. When we follow the footsteps of Jesus, this thought stands out over and over again. John the Baptist must be searched out and found far out in the wilderness, but Jesus was found among men. Simon Peter was busy with his nets, and Jesus came to where he was. Matthew sat at the seat of custom, and Jesus came to where he was. A demoniac was tormented in a graveyard and Jesus came to where he was. A paralyzed man by the pool of Bethesda was unable to walk, and Jesus came to where he was. Jairus's daughter was sick unto death, and Jesus came to where she was. Lazarus was already in the grave, and Jesus came to where he was. A widow would be under a huge cloud of grief and sorrow, as she followed the casket of her only son, and Jesus came to where she was. The disciples would find themselves in the worst storm of their lives, and Jesus came to where they were. Blind Bartimaeus would be consigned to the roadside at Jericho, and Jesus came to where he was. Tell the penitent thief on the cross that he must come down and take some far journey into the wilderness to search for a savior—but how beautiful the picture—the powerless and penitent; he turns his head and finds out that Jesus has come right where he was.

And I believe that on Tuesday morning, November 14, 2023, as Domenica was making the transition from this side of the dark glass to the other, Jesus was there. He came. Our hope rests on a promise keeper who said He would never leave us or forsake us but would be with us until the end.

In the 23rd Psalm David said, "Surely goodness and mercy shall *follow* me all the days of my life." Behind us always is the mercy of God. I guess in today's vernacular you could say it this way: "Mercy's got your back." Always offering the right guidance and direction, God's mercy is always available for us. It's described as everlasting; it's described as new every morning. But David said it follows all the days of our life. You see, I believe a transition takes place when we pass from this life into eternity. The psalmist said it this way in Psalm 89, speaking about God and His throne: "Mercy shall go before thy face." All the days of our lives mercy has followed us, but in that moment of our exit from this life, mercy trades places with us and goes before us, preceding us into the throne room of God—so the first thing God then sees is His mercy. The only hope that any of us have before His throne is the mercy of God. And thank God, that will be the lens through which He will view us in that day.

I believe in that moment mercy went before Minnie to the throne of God, and as He looked at her He saw the blood of Jesus that had covered her soul from the moment she accepted Him as her Savior at a young age. She could not outrun His love, she could not out-sin His mercy, and she could not outlast His goodness. And I can imagine back to the courtroom scene in heaven, when Minnie stood before the throne and Satan came to accuse her of all her sin, Jesus's voice thundered from the other side of the witness box, "She is mine!"

Let me tell you one more very important detail about her funeral services. Remember my prayer from the beginning that the Lord would use this for *her* good, for *His* glory, and for the salvation of many. Well, between the viewing, the funeral, and the gravesite services, there were about four hundred people in attendance. There were many of her high school friends, my old and new friends, coworkers, and family members, many of whom had never heard the true gospel. The Lord was glorified and His message of redemption went out for all of those souls to receive. We all prayed that hearts would be touched and lives changed, and I truly believe the Lord accomplished His work that day.

12

CLOSING THOUGHTS

I have learned so many truths through these years of grief and sorrow. Jesus has set before us many illustrations in nature and industry that provide for us examples of the trials and suffering we will experience in life and the blessings and treasures that can come from our hardship. This list is minor compared to the lessons all around us, and if you look hard enough, you too can start to see the handwriting of God everywhere you look:

> There are 40,000 pounds of string tension on a properly tuned piano in order for it to produce the deepest, most beautiful music.
> A goldsmith will continue to put his gold through the fire until the dross is completely removed and he can see his reflection. "A good refiner never leaves the crucible but . . . will sit down by it so the fire will not become even one degree too hot and possibly harm

the metal. And as soon as he skims the last bit of dross from the surface and sees his face reflected in the pure metal, he extinguishes the fire" (Malachi 3:3). (quoted in Cowman 407)

Extreme heat that burned down lush ancient forests produced coal. Coal requires great physical force and time to become priceless diamonds.

A diamond cutter will study a raw diamond for months, and with one sudden blow, which looks like it will destroy the raw diamond, he actually reveals its beauty. Sometimes, in the same way, God lets a stinging blow fall on your life. You bleed, feeling the pain, and your soul cries out in agony. At first you think the blow is an appalling mistake. But it is not, for you are the most precious jewel in the world to God. And He is the most skilled stonecutter in the universe. Someday you are to be a jewel adorning the crown of the King. (quoted in Cowman 159)

Friction creates power, forceful enough to even drive a massive ship or train, just as the mighty, raging water of Niagara Falls creates enough energy to power New York and into Canada.

The evening primrose is a flower that blooms only in the dark of night.

Wheat has to be crushed before it can be used to bake bread, but the farmer knows exactly when to stop crushing it (Isaiah 28:28).

People from all over the world go to Pebble Beach to collect the beautiful and unique rocks that have been pounded by the crashing waves and polished to perfection. However, other places along the California coast have quiet coves, sheltered from the beating surf, yet no one goes to these beaches to collect the rocks because they are unpolished, common, and ordinary.

Certain china is the finest because it has been put through the fire six different times, each time adding a layer of glaze, decoration, gold, and then a final fire to permanently fuse all the layers together, create its unique characteristics, and ensure the beauty and the durability of the china.

The heaviest pruning produces the fullest plants and the biggest, sweetest, and best fruit.

Trees planted by rivers are often washed over by flooding and pummeled by heavy winds, yet their roots dig in deep so they can withstand the harshest conditions.

The majestic cedars of Lebanon seemed to be mercilessly cut down and stripped of their lush branches, but they were used by Solomon to build the holy of holies, where the presence of the Lord would rest in Jerusalem.

Just as a butterfly needs the struggle to emerge from its cocoon in order for its wings to fill with fluid so it can fly, the Lord allows us to suffer and struggle in order to "fill our wings" so we will soar with a faith that can never be shaken.

I would like to leave you with the last few quotes, Scripture, and ideas that the Lord put on my heart to teach and encourage me, and I pray they will be a blessing for you as well.

"Faith does not say, 'I see this is good for me; therefore, God must have sent it.' Instead, faith declares, 'God sent it; therefore, it must be good for me'" (quoted in Cowman 178). This does not mean that what happens is always good but that the Lord has promised to use everything for our good. It also means that what may appear good doesn't necessarily mean it is good for us or that the Lord sent it.

The prophet Samuel, recognizing the hand of the Lord in his life and with the nation of Israel in spite of all the wars and seeming defeats, was able to declare in 1 Samuel 7:12, "Thus far the Lord has helped us." We too can look back over all the events of our lives, and if we look for God's hand we will definitely see His help woven throughout the fabric of our lives.

Finally, I would like to close with a list of extraordinary paradoxes found in the Bible. Only through a life lived in faith, where we've been beaten by the storms of life yet have emerged victorious, can we begin to understand how these could be true. "Only God can transform the wilderness into pasture, deserts into springs, perishable into imperishable, weakness into power, humiliation into glory, poverty into riches, mortality into immortality, this vile body into a resplendent body, my mourning into the oil of joy" (Elliot 104), a garment of praise for the spirit of heaviness, beauty for ashes, death to life, tragedy to triumph, and pain to redemption.

FAMILY GALLERY

This is the book I would read to Minnie when she was a child. After she passed, I found it in storage and was blown away by her little face in the yellow butterfly.

My neighbor's yard ornament that the Lord showed me on a particularly low day of mine after Minnie's passing.

The beautiful antique pin Minnie had picked up and wanted to buy just a few short weeks before Jesus took her home.

The little plastic yellow butterfly Minnie bought on vacation, which my friend found right after the Lord gave me my yellow butterfly confirmation.

My beautiful family on one of our fabulous road trips. We crossed forty-eight states together in our motorhome. From left are Steve, Joseph, Donna, Francesca, and Domenica (Minnie).

SCRIPTURE RESOURCE GUIDE

A dear friend gave me a beautiful journal for my birthday a few years back. The cover has a butterfly on it and the title *He Restores My Soul* (Psalm 23:3). On the back she had the inscription written, "A child of God, a woman of faith, a warrior for Christ." After I finish reading through the Bible (I try to do it every year), I pick out something to highlight and journal. This past year I decided to use this journal to write what I titled "2023 Promises, Encouragement, Blessings." My sweet Minnie passed while I was in this process, and I know it was no mistake that the Lord had me soaking in His promises, encouragement, and blessings at the time. I want to take the remainder of our time together to list these out for you, and I want you to hold tightly to these as your own because God wrote them just for you, as He wrote them just for me. Let this section be your go-to guide for daily help and hope. Some promises will speak to you more than others, and some others during different seasons of your life, but if you're reading this book, I sense you are in the midst of a raging storm and need rest and hope from the one who calms the seas. Claim His promises for yourself and for your family, be renewed by the encouragement as the Lord cheers you on to the finish line, and bask in His blessings as you savor every word that He spoke over you. Let Him restore your soul.

Genesis 15:1—I am your shield, your exceedingly great reward.

Genesis 18:14—Is anything too hard for the Lord?

Genesis 35:3—God, who answered me in the day of my distress and has been with me in the way which I have gone.

Genesis 50:20—You meant evil against me; but God meant it for good, in order to bring it about as it is this day, to save many people alive.

Exodus 14:13–14—Do not be afraid. Stand still and see the salvation of the Lord, which He will accomplish for you today. . . . The Lord will fight for you, and you shall hold your peace.

Exodus 15:2—The Lord is my strength and my song, and He has become my salvation.

Exodus 15:26—I am the Lord who heals you.

Exodus 33:14—And He said, "My Presence will go with you, and I will give you rest."

Exodus 34:6–7—And the Lord passed before him and proclaimed, "The Lord, the Lord God, merciful and gracious, longsuffering, and abounding in goodness and truth, keeping mercy for thousands, forgiving iniquity and transgression and sin."

Exodus 2:24—So God heard their groaning, and God remembered His covenant.

Exodus 3:12—So He said, "I will certainly be with you."

Numbers 6:24–26—The Lord bless you and keep you; the Lord make His face shine upon you, and be gracious to you; the Lord life up His countenance upon you, and give you peace.

Deuteronomy 3:22—You must not fear them, for the Lord your God Himself fights for you.

Deuteronomy 20:3–4—"Today you are on the verge of battle with your enemies. Do not let your heart faint, do not be afraid, and do not tremble or be terrified because of them; for the Lord your God is He who goes with you, to fight against your enemies, to save you."

Deuteronomy 23:5—The Lord your God turned the curse into a blessing for you, because the Lord Your God loves you.

Deuteronomy 31:8—The Lord, He is the One who goes before you. He will be with you, He will not leave you nor forsake you; do not fear nor be dismayed.

Deuteronomy 32:4—He is the rock, His work is perfect, for all His ways are justice, a God of truth and without injustice; righteous and upright is He.

Deuteronomy 33:27—The eternal God is your refuge, and underneath are the everlasting arms.

Joshua 1:9—Have I not commanded you? Be strong and of good courage; do not be afraid, nor be dismayed; for the Lord your God is with you wherever you go.

Joshua 23:14—You know in all your hearts and in all your souls that not one thing has failed of all the good things which the Lord your God spoke concerning you.

1 Samuel 14:6—Nothing restrains the Lord from saving by many or by few.

2 Samuel 22:7, 20—In my distress I called upon the Lord, and cried out to my God; He heard my voice from His temple, and my cry entered His ears. . . . He also brought me out into a broad place; He delivered me because He delighted in me.

2 Samuel 22:31—As for God, His way is perfect; the word of the Lord is proven; He is a shield to all who trust in Him.

2 Samuel 22:33—God is my strength and power, and He makes my way perfect.

1 Kings 8:56—There has not failed one word of all His good promise.

1 Chronicles 21:13—Please let me fall into the hand of the Lord, for His mercies are very great; but do not let me fall into the hand of man.

2 Chronicles 14:11—Lord, it is nothing for You to help, whether with many or with those who have no power; help us, O Lord our God, for we rest on You, and in Your name…

2 Chronicles 16:9—The eyes of the Lord run to and fro throughout the whole earth, to show Himself strong on behalf of those whose heart is loyal to Him.

2 Chronicles 20:12, 15, 17—We have no power against this great multitude . . . nor do we know what to do, but our eyes are upon You. Thus says the Lord to you: "Do not be afraid nor dismayed . . . for the battle is not yours, but God's. You will not need to fight in this battle. Position yourselves, stand still and see the salvation of the Lord, who is with you, O Judah and Jerusalem!" Do not fear or be dismayed; tomorrow go out against them, for the Lord is with you.

2 Chronicles 30:9—The Lord your God is gracious and merciful, and will not turn His face from you if you return to Him.

Ezra 8:23—So we fasted and entreated our God for this, and He answered our prayer.

Ezra 9:13—You our God have punished us less than our iniquities deserve, and have given us such deliverance as this.

Nehemiah 4:14—Do not be afraid of them. Remember the Lord, great and awesome, and fight for your brethren, your sons, your daughters, your wives, and your houses.

Nehemiah 8:10—Do not sorrow, for the joy of the Lord is your strength.

Nehemiah 9:17, 28, 31—You are God, ready to pardon, gracious and merciful, slow to anger, abundant in kindness. . . . When they returned and cried out to You, You heard from heaven; and many times You delivered them according to Your mercies. . . . In Your great mercy You did not utterly consume them nor forsake them; for You are God, gracious and merciful.

Nehemiah 13:2—Our God turned the curse into a blessing.

Job 1:21—The Lord gave, and the Lord has taken away; blessed be the name of the Lord.

Job 2:10—Shall we indeed accept good from God, and shall we not accept adversity?

Job 5:17–18—Behold, happy is the man whom God corrects; therefore do not despise the chastening of the Almighty. For He bruises, but He binds up; He wounds, but His hands make whole.

Job 13:15—Though He slay me, yet will I trust Him.

Job 14:5—Since his days are determined, the number of his months is with You; You have appointed his limits, so that he cannot pass. (*This has given me such great comfort, knowing that nothing I could have done would have saved Minnie's life that day. Before she was born, the Lord knew when her last breath would be.*)

Job 19: 25–26—I know that my Redeemer lives, and He shall stand at last on the earth; and after my skin is destroyed, this I know, that in my flesh I shall see God,

Job 23:10—He knows the way that I take; when He has tested me, I shall come forth as gold.

Job 33:28—He will redeem his soul from going down to the Pit, and his life shall see the light.

Job 42:2—I know that You can do everything, and that no purpose of Yours can be withheld from You.

Psalm 1:1–3—Blessed is the one [whose] delight is in the law of the Lord, and who meditates on his law day and night. That person is like a tree planted by streams of water, which yields its fruit in season and whose leaf does not wither—whatever they do prospers.

Psalm 2:12—Blessed are all those who put their trust in Him.

Psalm 3:3–4—You, O Lord, are a shield for me, my glory and the One who lifts up my head. I cried to the Lord with my voice, and He heard me from His holy hill.

Psalm 4:1, 3, 7–8—You have relieved me in my distress. . . . The Lord will hear when I call to Him. . . . You have put gladness in my heart. . . . I will both lie down in peace and sleep.

Psalm 5:12—You, O Lord, will bless the righteous; with favor You will surround him as with a shield.

Psalm 6:8–9—The Lord has heard the voice of my weeping. The Lord has heard my supplication. The Lord will receive my prayer.

Psalm 8:4—What is man that You are mindful of him, and the son of man that You visit him?

Psalm 9:4, 9—You have maintained my right and my cause. . . . The Lord also will be a refuge for the oppressed, a refuge in times of trouble.

Psalm 9:10—Those who know Your name will put their trust in You; for You, Lord, have not forsaken those who seek You.

Psalm 13:6—I sing to the Lord because He has dealt bountifully with me.

Psalm 16:7—My heart also instructs me in the night seasons.

Psalm 16:8–9—I have set the Lord always before me; because He is at my right hand I shall not be moved. Therefore my heart is glad, and my glory rejoices; my flesh also will rest in hope.

Psalm 16:11—You will show me the path of life; in Your presence is fullness of joy; at your right hand are pleasures forevermore.

Psalm 18:2, 6—The Lord is my rock and my fortress and my deliverer; my God, my strength in whom I will trust, my shield and the horn of my salvation, my stronghold. . . . In my distress I called upon the Lord, and cried out to my God; He heard my voice from his temple, and my cry came before Him, even to His ears.

Psalm 18:16, 19—He sent from above, He took me; He drew me out of many waters. . . . He also brought me out into a broad place; He delivered me because He delighted in me. (*This was the scripture in my daily reading on the one-month mark of Minnie's passing. God was reiterating to me again that He had rescued her!*)

Psalm 18:28–31—You will light my lamp; the Lord my God will enlighten my darkness. For by You I can run against a troop, by my God I can leap over a wall. As for God, His way is perfect; the word of the Lord is proven; He is a shield to all who trust in Him. For who is God, except the Lord? And who is a rock except our God?

Psalm 18:35–36—You have also given me the shield of Your salvation; Your right hand has held me up, Your gentleness has made me great. You enlarged my path under me, so my feet did not slip.

Psalm 18:39—You have armed me with strength for the battle.

Psalm 22:24—When he cried to Him, He heard.

Psalm 23:4—I will fear no evil; for You are with me; Your rod and Your staff, they comfort me.

Psalm 27:1, 5—The Lord is my light and salvation; whom shall I fear? The Lord is the strength of my life; of whom shall I be afraid? . . . For in the time of trouble He shall hide me in His pavilion; in the secret place of His Tabernacle He shall hide me; He shall set me high upon a rock.

Psalm 27:13–14—I would have lost heart, unless I had *believed* that I would see the goodness of the Lord in the land of the living. Wait on the Lord; be of good courage, and He shall strengthen your heart; wait, I say, on the Lord! (*emphasis added*)

Psalm 28:7—The Lord is my strength and my shield; my heart trusted in Him, and I am helped; therefore, my heart greatly rejoices.

Psalm 29:11—The Lord will give strength to His people. The Lord will bless His people with peace.

Psalm 30:2–3—O Lord my God, I cried out to you and you healed me. O Lord, you brought my soul up from the grave; You have kept me alive, that I should not go down to the pit.

Psalm 30:5, 11—Weeping may endure for a night, but joy comes in the morning. . . . You have turned for me my mourning into dancing; you have put off my sackcloth and clothed me with gladness.

Psalm 31:14–15—As for me, I trust in You, O Lord; I say, "You are my God." My times are in Your hand.

Psalm 31:19—Oh, how great is Your goodness, which You have laid up for those who fear You, which You have prepared for those who trust in You in the presence of the sons of men!

Psalm 31:20—You shall hide them in the secret place of Your presence.

Psalm 31:22–24—I said in my haste, "I am cut off from before Your eyes"; Nevertheless You heard the voice of my supplications when I cried out to You. Oh, love the Lord, all you His saints, For the Lord preserves the faithful. . . . Be of good courage, and He shall strengthen your heart, all you who hope in the Lord.

Psalm 32:7–8—You are my hiding place; You shall preserve me from trouble; You shall surround me with songs of deliverance. I will instruct you and teach you in the way you should go; I will guide you with My eye.

Psalm 32:10—He who trusts in the Lord, mercy shall surround him.

Psalm 33:18–20—Behold, the eye of the Lord is on those who fear Him, on those who hope in His mercy, to deliver their soul from death, and to keep them alive in famine. Our soul waits for the Lord; He is our help and our shield.

Psalm 34:4—I sought the Lord, and He heard me, and delivered me from all my fears.

Psalm 34:8, 10—Oh, taste and see that the Lord is good; blessed is the man who trust in Him! . . . Those who seek the Lord shall not lack any good thing.

Psalm 34:15, 17—The eyes of the Lord are on the righteous, and His ears are open to their cry. . . . The righteous cry out, and the Lord hears, and delivers them out of all their troubles.

Psalm 34:18—The Lord is close to the brokenhearted and saves those who are crushed in spirit (NIV).

Psalm 34:19—Many are the afflictions of the righteous, but the Lord delivers him out of them all.

Psalm 37:3–5, 7—*Trust* in the Lord, and do good; dwell in the land, and feed on His faithfulness. *Delight* yourself also in the Lord, and He shall give you the desires of your heart. *Commit* your way to the Lord, *trust* also in Him, and He shall bring in to pass. . . . *Rest* in the Lord, and wait patiently for Him (*emphasis added*).

Psalm 37:23–24—The steps of a good man are ordered by the Lord, and He delights in his way. Though he fall, he shall not be utterly cast down; for the Lord upholds him with His hand.

Psalm 37:39–40—But the salvation of the righteous is from the Lord; He is their strength in the time of trouble. And the Lord shall help them and deliver them; He shall deliver them from the wicked, and save them, because they trust in Him.

Psalm 39:7—And now, Lord, what do I wait for? My hope is in You.

Psalm 40:1–3—I waited patiently for the Lord; and He inclined to me, and heard my cry. He also brought me up out of a horrible pit, out of the miry clay, and set my feet upon a rock, and established my steps. He has put a new song in my mouth—praise to our God; many will see it and fear, and will trust in the Lord.

Psalm 40:17—I am poor and needy; yet the Lord thinks upon me. You are my help and my deliverer; do not delay, O my God.

Psalm 42:5—Why are you cast down, O my soul? And why are you disquieted within me? Hope in God, for I shall yet praise Him for the help of His countenance.

Psalm 42:8—The Lord will command His lovingkindness in the daytime, and in the night His song shall be with me—a prayer to the God of my life.

Psalm 46:1–2, 5—God is our refuge and strength, a very present help in trouble. Therefore we will not fear. . . . God is in the midst of her, she shall not be moved; God shall help her, just at the break of dawn.

Psalm 46:10—Be still, and know that I am God. *(When someone is taking our picture, we need to be still until our image is captured. When God tells us to be still, it is so we can conform to the likeness of Jesus. This cannot happen while we busy ourselves constantly and try to work things out on our own.)*

Psalm 50:15—Call upon Me in the day of trouble; I will deliver you, and you shall glorify Me.

Psalm 51:1—Have mercy upon me, O God, according to Your lovingkindness; according to the multitude of Your tender mercies, blot out my transgressions.

Psalm 54:4—Behold, God is my helper; the Lord is with those who uphold my life.

Psalm 54:7—He has delivered me out of all trouble.

Psalm 55:16—As for me, I will call upon God, and the Lord shall save me.

Psalm 55:22—Cast your cares on the Lord and He will sustain you; He will never let the righteous be shaken (NIV).

Psalm 56:3, 8, 11—Whenever I am afraid, I will trust in You. . . . You number my wanderings; put my tears into Your bottle; are they not in Your book? . . . In God I have put my trust; I will not be afraid. What can man do to me?

Psalm 57:1–3—Be merciful to me, O God, be merciful to me! For my soul trusts in You; and in the shadow of Your wings I will make my refuge, until these calamities have passed by. I will cry out to God Most High, to God who performs all things for me. He shall send from heaven and save me; He reproaches the one who would swallow me up. *Selah*. God shall send for His mercy and His truth.

Psalm 60:11—Give us help from trouble, for the help of man is useless. (*When I read this verse I realized that I was looking for the help of man, with all the doctors, medications, facilities, and so on. I realized at that moment that these had taken the rightful place of God, and I needed to refocus and place my baby in His hands alone, knowing He would direct my steps.*)

Psalm 61:2—When my heart is overwhelmed; lead me to the rock that is higher than I.

Psalm 62:1–2—Truly my soul silently waits for God; from Him comes my salvation. He only is my rock and my salvation; He is my defense; I shall not be greatly moved.

Psalm 62:5–7—My soul, wait silently for God alone, for my expectation is from Him. He only is my rock and my salvation; He is my defense; I shall not be moved. In God is my salvation and my glory; the rock of my strength, and my refuge, is in God.

Psalm 63:3–4, 7–8—Because Your lovingkindness is better than life, my lips shall praise You. Thus I will bless You while I live; I will lift up my hands in Your name. . . . Because You have been my help, therefore in the shadow of Your wings I will rejoice. My soul follows close behind You; Your right hand upholds me.

Psalm 65:11—You crown the year with Your goodness, and Your paths drip with abundance.

Psalm 66:12—We went through fire and through water; but You brought us out to rich fulfillment.

Psalm 66:20—Blessed be God, who has not turned away my prayer, nor His mercy from me!

Psalm 68:19–20—Blessed be the Lord, who daily loads us with benefits, the God of our salvation! *Selah*. Our God is the God of salvation; and to God the Lord belong escapes from death.

Psalm 69:32—The humble shall see this and be glad; and you who seek God, your hearts shall live.

Psalm 71:5–6, 14–16—You are my hope, O Lord God; You are my trust from my youth. By You I have been upheld from birth. . . . I will hope continually, and will praise You yet more and more. My mouth shall tell of Your righteousness and Your salvation all the day, for I do not know their limits. I will go in the strength of the Lord God.

Psalm 71:20—You, who have shown me great and severe troubles, shall revive me again, and bring me up again from the depths of the earth.

Psalm 73:23–24, 26, 28—Nevertheless I am continually with You; You hold me by your right hand. You will guide me with Your counsel, and afterward receive me to glory. . . . My flesh and my heart fail; but God is the strength of my heart and my portion forever. . . . But it is good for me to draw near to God; I have put my trust in the Lord God, that I may declare all Your works.

Psalm 77:10–12 (*This has been and sometimes still is me. My soul is in anguish; my tears fall without consolation.*) And I said, "This is my anguish; *but I will remember* the years of the right hand of the Most High." I will remember the works of the Lord; surely I will remember Your wonders of old. I will also meditate on all Your work, and talk of Your deeds. (emphasis added. *Whenever I begin to think about who God is and what He has done, He comforts my soul.*)

Psalm 78:38—He, being full of compassion, forgave their iniquity, and did not destroy them. Yes, many a time He turned His anger away, and did not stir up all His wrath.

Psalm 84:5–7—Blessed is the man whose strength is in You, whose heart is set on pilgrimage. As they pass through the Valley of Baca [*weeping*], they make it a spring; the rain also covers it with pools. They go from strength to strength.

Psalm 84:11—The Lord God is a sun and shield; the Lord will give grace and glory; no good thing will He withhold from those who walk uprightly.

Psalm 86:7—In the day of my trouble I will call upon You, for You will answer me.

Psalm 86:13, 15—Great is Your mercy toward me, and You have delivered my soul from the depths of Sheol. . . . But You, O Lord, are a God full of compassion, and gracious, longsuffering and abundant in mercy and truth. (*This gives me so much comfort for my Minnie. God is all He says He is!*)

Psalm 89:8–9—O Lord God of hosts, who is mighty like You, O Lord? Your faithfulness also surrounds You. You rule the raging of the sea; when its waves rise, You still them.

Psalm 89:14—Righteousness and justice are the foundation of Your throne; mercy and truth go before Your face.

Psalm 89:32–33—I will punish their transgression with the rod, and their iniquity with stripes. Nevertheless My lovingkindness I will not utterly take from him, nor allow My faithfulness to fail. (*God says, like an earthly father, that He punishes those He loves, and He does it to preserve our souls. The Lord punished Minnie because He loves her and was faithful to her, even unto her death.*)

Psalm 91—the entire chapter but specifically verses 1–2, 11, 14–16—He who dwells in the secret place of the Most High shall abide under the shadow of the Almighty. I will say of the Lord, "He is my refuge and my fortress; my God, in Him I will trust." . . . For He shall give His angels charge over you, to keep you in all your ways. . . . "Because he has set his love upon Me, therefore I will deliver him; I will set him on high, because he has known My name. He shall call upon Me, and I will answer him; I will be with him in trouble; I will deliver him and honor him. With long life I will satisfy him, and show him My salvation."

Psalm 94:19—In the multitude of my anxieties within me, Your comforts delight my soul.

Psalm 103—*Read it again in its entirety, paying careful attention to verses 2–5, 8–12, 17.* Bless the Lord, O my soul, and forget not all His benefits: Who *forgives* all your iniquities, Who *heals* all your diseases, Who *redeems* your life from destruction, Who *crowns* you with lovingkindness and tender mercies, Who *satisfies* your mouth with good things, so that your youth is renewed like the eagle's *(emphasis added)*. The Lord is merciful and gracious, slow to anger, and abounding in mercy. He will not always strive with us, nor will He keep His anger forever. He has not dealt with us according to our sins, nor punished us according to our iniquities. For as the heavens are high above the earth, so great is His mercy toward those who fear Him; as far as the east is from the west, so far has He removed our transgressions from us. But the mercy of the Lord is from everlasting to everlasting on those who fear Him, and His righteousness to children's children.

Psalm 107—I won't include the whole chapter, but I want you to take time to read it and take note of all the times it says, "Then they cried out to the Lord in their trouble, and He saved them out of their distress." This chapter is one of desperation and deliverance!

Psalm 107:35—He turns a wilderness into pools of water, and dry land into water springs.

Psalm 111:4, 7—He has made His wonderful works to be remembered; the Lord is gracious and full of compassion. . . . The works of His hands are verity and justice; and His precepts are sure.

Psalm 112:1, 7–8—Blessed is the man who fears the Lord, who delights greatly in His commandments. . . . He will not be afraid of evil tidings; his heart is steadfast, trusting in the Lord. His heart is established; he will not be afraid.

Psalm 116:1–2—I love the Lord, because He has heard my voice and my supplications. Because He has inclined His ear to me, therefore I will call upon Him as long as I live.

Psalm 116:15—Precious in the sight of the Lord is the death of His saints.

Psalm 118:5—I called on the Lord in distress; the Lord answered me and set me in a broad place.

Psalm 118:8—It is better to trust in the Lord than to put confidence in man.

Psalm 118:24—This is the day the Lord has made; we will rejoice and be glad in it.

Psalm 119:49–50—Remember the word to Your servant, upon which You have caused me to hope. This is my comfort in my affliction, for Your word has given me life. (*This is the passage I read the morning I found my sweet girl. God is so good to have given me this reassurance, knowing I would need to cling to this hope.*)

Psalm 119:67, 71—Before I was afflicted I went astray, but now I keep Your word. . . . It is good for me that I have been afflicted, that I may learn Your statutes.

Psalm 119:105—Your word is a lamp to my feet and a light to my path.

Psalm 119:114—You are my hiding place and my shield; I hope in Your word.

Psalm 119:160—The entirety of Your word is truth, and every one of Your righteous judgments endures forever. (*Yes! We can count on the sure promises of our God.*)

Psalm 120:1—In my distress I cried to the Lord, and He heard me.

Psalm 121:1–3—I will lift up my eyes to the hills—from whence comes my help? My help comes from the Lord, who made heaven and earth. He will not allow your foot to be moved; He who keeps you will not slumber.

Psalm 121:7—The Lord shall preserve you from all evil; He shall preserve your soul. (*Remember the message from Pastor Jack Hibbs's podcast? He will preserve our souls, even if it means our physical destruction.*)

Psalm 126:5—Those who sow in tears shall reap in joy.

Psalm 130:5—I wait for the Lord, my soul waits, and in His word I do hope.

Psalm 130:7—With the Lord there is mercy, and with Him is abundant redemption. (*Oh, my goodness! The sweet and precious mercy of the Lord, abundantly redeeming our souls!*)

Psalm 138:3—In the day when I cried out, You answered me, and made me bold with strength in my soul.

Psalm 138:7—Though I walk in the midst of trouble, You will revive me.

Psalm 138:8—The Lord will *perfect* that which concerns me; Your mercy, O Lord, endures forever; do not forsake the works of Your hands (*emphasis added*).

Psalm 139:5–6—You have hedged me behind and before, and laid Your hand upon me. Such knowledge is too wonderful for me; it is high; I cannot attain it.

Psalm 139:14—I will praise You, for I am fearfully and wonderfully made; marvelous are Your works, and that my soul knows very well. (*He made each of us with wonderful care and love.*)

Psalm 139:16—In Your book they all were written, the days fashioned for me, when as yet there were none of them. (*This is another verse that gives me such reassurance, that no matter what I could have done that day, the Lord knew Minnie's last breath on earth long before she ever took her first one. This verse has removed all "what if's" because I know in my heart that her days were fashioned for her before she was ever born.)*

Psalm 141:8—My eyes are upon You, O God the Lord; in You I take refuge; do not leave my soul destitute.

Psalm 142:3—When my spirit was overwhelmed within me, then You knew my path.

Psalm 143:4, 8—My spirit is overwhelmed within me; my heart within me is distressed. . . . Cause me to hear Your lovingkindness in the morning, for in You do I trust; cause me to know the way in which I should walk, for I lift up my soul to You.

Psalm 144:1–2—Blessed be the Lord my Rock . . . my lovingkindness and my fortress, my high tower and my deliverer, my shield and the One in whom I take refuge.

Psalm 144:3—Lord, what is man, that You take knowledge of him? Or the son of man, that You are mindful of him?

Psalm 145:8–9—The Lord is gracious and full of compassion, slow to anger and great in mercy. The Lord is good to all, and His tender mercies are over all His works.

Psalm 145:17–19—The Lord is righteous in all His ways, gracious in all His works. The Lord is near to all who call upon Him, to all who call upon Him in truth. He will fulfill the desire of those who fear Him; He will also hear their cry and save them.

Psalm 147:3—He heals the brokenhearted and binds up their wounds.

Psalm 147:11—The Lord takes pleasure in those who fear Him, in those who hope in His mercy.

Proverbs 1:33—Whoever listens to me will dwell safely, and will be secure, without fear of evil.

Proverbs 2:7–8—He is a shield to those who walk uprightly. He guards the path of the justice and preserves the way of His saints. (*Let me interject that all who belong to God are called His saints! See Romans 1:7; 1 Corinthians 1:2; 2 Corinthians 1:1; Colossians 1:2; Ephesians 1:1—just to name a few!*)

Proverbs 3:5–6—Trust in the Lord with all your heart and lean not on your own understanding. In all your ways acknowledge Him, and He shall direct your paths.

Proverbs 3:7–8—Fear the Lord and depart from evil. It will be health to your flesh and strength to your bones.

Proverbs 3:12—Whom the Lord loves He corrects.

Proverbs 3:24–26—When you lie down, you will not be afraid; yes, you will lie down and your sleep will be sweet. Do not be afraid of sudden terror, nor of trouble from the wicked when it comes; for the Lord will be your confidence, and will keep your foot from being caught.

Proverbs 3:33–35—He blesses the home of the just. . . . [He] gives grace to the humble. The wise shall inherit glory.

Proverbs 16:20—He who heeds the word wisely will find good, and whoever trusts in the Lord, happy is he.

Proverbs 18:10—The name of the Lord is a strong tower; the righteous run into it and are safe.

Proverbs 19:21—Many are the plans in a person's heart, but it is the Lord's purpose that prevails (NIV).

Proverbs 23:18—For surely there is a hereafter, and your hope will not be cut off.

Ecclesiastes 3:11—He has made everything beautiful in its time.

Isaiah 5:25; 9:12, 17, 21; 10:4—For all this His anger is not turned away, but His hand is stretched out still. (*Wow! This is verse after verse, identical wording, of how God's people turned their backs on Him time after time; yet His love and mercy triumphed*).

Isaiah 9:6—Unto us a Child is born, unto us a Son is given; and the government will be upon His shoulder. And His name will be called Wonderful, Counselor, Mighty God, Everlasting Father, Prince of Peace. (*Only Jesus!*)

Isaiah 14:24—The Lord of hosts has sworn, saying, "Surely, as I have thought, so it shall come to pass, and as I have purposed, so it shall stand."

Isaiah 25:8—He will swallow up death forever, and the Lord God will wipe away tears from all faces. (*Oh, how I long for that day!*)

Isaiah 26:3, 4—You will keep him in perfect peace, whose mind is stayed on You, because he trusts in You. Trust in the Lord forever, for in YAH, the Lord, is everlasting strength.

Isaiah 30:15—Thus says the Lord God, the Holy One of Israel: "In returning and rest you shall be saved; in quietness and confidence shall be your strength."

Isaiah 30:18—The Lord will wait, that He may be gracious to you; and therefore He will be exalted, that He may have mercy on you. For the Lord is a God of justice; blessed are all those who wait for Him.

Isaiah 30:21—Your ears shall hear a word behind you, saying, "This is the way, walk in it," whenever you turn to the right hand or whenever you turn to the left.

Isaiah 32:17—The work of righteousness will be peace, and the effect of righteousness, quietness and assurance forever.

Isaiah 35:10—The ransomed of the Lord shall return, and come to Zion with singing, with everlasting joy on their heads. They shall obtain joy and gladness, and sorrow and sighing shall flee away. (*Do you yearn for that day as much as I do?*)

Isaiah 40:28–31—Have you not known? Have you not heard? The everlasting God, the Lord, the Creator of the ends of the earth, neither faints nor is weary. His understanding is unsearchable. He gives power to the weak, and to those who have no might He increases strength. Even the youths shall faint and be weary, and the young men shall utterly fall, but those who wait on the Lord shall renew their strength; They shall mount up with wings like eagles, they shall run and not be weary, they shall walk and not faint.

Isaiah 41:10—Fear not, for I am with you; be not dismayed, for I am your God. I will strengthen you, yes, I will help you, I will uphold you with my righteous right hand.

Isaiah 43:2—When you pass through the waters, I will be with you; and through the rivers, they shall not overflow you. When you walk through the fire, you shall not be burned, nor shall the flame scorch you.

Isaiah 43:19—Behold, I will do a new thing, now it shall spring forth; shall you not know it? I will even make a road in the wilderness and rivers in the desert.

Isaiah 43:25—I, even I, am He who blots out your transgressions for My own sake; and I will not remember your sins.

Isaiah 46:4—Even to your old age I am he, and even to gray hairs I will carry you! I have made, and I will bear; even I will carry, and will deliver you.

Isaiah 46:9–11—I am God, and there is no other; I am God, and there is none like Me, declaring the end from the beginning, and from ancient times things that are not yet done, saying, "My counsel shall stand, and I will do all My pleasure," calling a bird of prey from the east, the man who executes My counsel, from a far country. Indeed I have spoken it; I will also bring it to pass. I have purposed it; I will also do it. (*Only the Lord is timeless and can see the beginning and the end. He declares things that haven't happened yet, and they come to pass with 100-percent accuracy, even bringing animals and people into obedience to His plan. This may make some people mad, but for me it brings so much comfort.*)

Isaiah 48:10—Behold, I have refined you, but not as silver; I have tested you in the furnace of affliction.

Isaiah 50:2—Is My hand shortened at all that it cannot redeem? Or have I no power to deliver?

Isaiah 54:7–8—"For a mere moment I have forsaken you, but with great mercies I will gather you. With a little wrath I hid My face from you for a moment; but with everlasting kindness I will have mercy on you," says the Lord, your Redeemer.

Isaiah 55:8–9—"My thoughts are not your thoughts, nor are your ways My ways," says the Lord. "For as the heavens are higher than the earth, so are My ways higher than your ways, and My thoughts than your thoughts. (*Because of this, we can trust Him completely, even if it doesn't seem that He could make anything good out of our circumstances.*)

Isaiah 55:11—So shall My word be that goes forth from My mouth; it shall not return to Me void, but it shall accomplish what I please, and it shall prosper in the thing for which I sent it. (*What a beautiful promise this is! This says that what God speaks or has recorded in His Word will accomplish what He intends it to accomplish*).

Isaiah 59:1—Behold, the Lord's hand is not shortened, that it cannot save; nor His ear heavy, that it cannot hear.

Isaiah 61:1–3—The Spirit of the Lord God is upon Me, because the Lord has anointed Me to preach good tidings to the poor; He has sent Me to heal the brokenhearted, to proclaim liberty to the captives, and the opening of the prison to those who are bound; to proclaim the acceptable year of the Lord, and the day of vengeance of our God; to comfort all who mourn, To console those who mourn in Zion, To give them beauty for ashes, The oil of joy for mourning, The garment of praise for the spirit of heaviness; That they may be called trees of righteousness, The planting of the Lord, that He may be glorified. (*This is one of the most beautiful Old Testament prophecies about the coming Messiah, Jesus. This tells of His mission here on earth. I highlighted those things that I so desperately need, and as we've seen many times now, He will do as He promised.*)

Isaiah 64:4—Since the beginning of the world men have not heard nor perceived by ear, nor has the eye seen any God besides You,

Who acts for the one who waits for Him. (*Wow—read this again! The God of the universe acts on behalf of those who wait for Him! This is the loving, gracious, merciful, and very real God we serve.*)

Jeremiah 9:24—I am the Lord, exercising lovingkindness, judgment, and righteousness in the earth.

Jeremiah 17:7–8—Blessed is the man who trusts in the Lord, and whose hope is the Lord. For he shall be like a tree planted by the waters, which spreads out its roots by the river, and will not fear when heat comes; but its leaf will be green, and will not be anxious in the year of drought, nor will cease from yielding fruit.

Jeremiah 17:14—Heal me, O Lord, and I shall be healed; save me, and I shall be saved.

Jeremiah 18:6—Look, as the clay is in the potter's hand, so are you in My hand.

Jeremiah 29:11—For I know the plans I have for you," declares the Lord, "plans to prosper you and not to harm you, plans to give you hope and a future (NIV). (*As I mentioned before, this is the life verse our pastor, through the Holy Spirit, chose for Minnie when we dedicated her as a baby. I reminded her of this verse often. I know she felt that her life was one obstacle after the next, and she probably felt hopeless and could not see a future, but God knew all along that this hope and future meant taking her out of her pain and struggles.*)

Jeremiah 29:12–13—Then you will call upon Me and go and pray to Me, and I will listen to you. And you will seek Me and find Me, when you search for Me with all your heart. (*Although verse 11 was Minnie's life verse, these two following verses are for me! The Lord does listen because I am truly seeking Him with all my heart. Another amazing promise from the Lord.*)

Jeremiah 31:3—Yes, I have loved you with an everlasting love; therefore with lovingkindness I have drawn you.

Jeremiah 32:27—Behold, I am the Lord, the God of all flesh. Is there anything too hard for Me?

Jeremiah 33:3—Call to Me, and I will answer you, and show you great and mighty things, which you do not know.

Lamentations 3:21–26—This I recall to my mind, therefore I have hope. Through the Lord's mercies we are not consumed, because His compassions fail not. They are new every morning; Great is Your faithfulness. "The Lord is my portion," says my soul, "Therefore I hope in Him!" The Lord is good to those who wait for Him, to the soul who seeks Him. It is good that one should hope and wait quietly for the salvation of the Lord.

Lamentations 3:31–32—The Lord will not cast off forever. Though He causes grief, yet He will show compassion according to the multitude of His mercies. (*Do you see the theme of these last two passages? Compassion and mercy! This is our God!*)

Lamentations 3:55, 57—I called on Your name, O Lord, from the lowest pit. . . . You drew near on the day I called on You, and said, "Do not fear!" (*Obviously I wasn't there when Minnie went to be with Jesus, but I imagine that as she was taking her last breath, she cried out to Jesus from her lowest pit, and He drew her out, comforted her, and walked her through death into her new eternal life.*)

Daniel 3:17–18—If that is the case, our God whom we serve is able to deliver us from the burning fiery furnace. . . . But if not (*I wrote in my journal about this passage, knowing that God was able to deliver my Minnie from her earthly torment. However, I had to have the conversation with myself that would I still trust Him—"but if not."*)

Daniel 6:26–27—He is the living God, and steadfast forever; He delivers and rescues, and He works signs and wonders in heaven and on earth.

Hosea 14:4—I will heal their backsliding, I will love them freely, for My anger has turned away from him.

Joel 2:25—So I will restore to you the years that the swarming locust has eaten, the crawling locust, the consuming locust, and the chewing locust (*I am still waiting for this promise to be fulfilled. The "locust" has consumed the last several years of my life—tearing down, devouring, destroying. But God has promised that He will restore those years. Will I see that here in my lifetime? Perhaps, but if not, I know He will more than restore once I get to my eternal home.*)

Joel 2:32—Whoever calls on the name of the Lord shall be saved. (*This is still true today! That's why Paul reiterated it in Romans 10:13.*)

Jonah 2:6–7—You have brought up my life from the pit, O Lord, my God. When my soul fainted within me, I remembered the Lord; and my prayer went up to You, into Your holy temple.

Jonah 4:2—I know that You are a gracious and merciful God, slow to anger and abundant in lovingkindness, One who relents from doing harm.

Micah 7:7—I will look to the Lord; I will wait for the God of my salvation; my God will hear me.

Micah 7:18–19—Who is a God like You, pardoning iniquity and passing over the transgression of the remnant of His heritage? He does not retain His anger forever, because He delights in mercy. He will again have compassion on us, and will subdue our iniquities. You will cast all our sins into the depths of the sea. (*Mercy and compassion! This is the overall theme of the entire Bible: God's mercy and compassion on a sinful world—His plan of saving mankind even from the very beginning in Genesis 3:15*).

Nahum 1:7—The Lord is good, a stronghold in the day of trouble; and He knows those who trust in Him.

Habakkuk 2:4—The just shall live by faith.

Habakkuk 3:17–18—Though the fig tree may not blossom, nor fruit be on the vines; though the labor of the olive may fail, and the fields yield no food; though the flock may be cut off from the fold and there be no herd in the stalls—Yet I will rejoice in the Lord, I will joy in the God of my salvation (*Everything he lists here is disastrous; his livelihood and sustenance are gone—yet he never turns on God and instead continues to rejoice in Him.*)

Zephaniah 3:17—The Lord your God in your midst, the Mighty One, will save; He will rejoice over you with gladness, He will quiet you with His love, He will rejoice over you with singing. (*During this time of intense grief, questioning, and sadness, I can say I have felt Him quiet me with His love, and it is truly a feeling like no other. It is like being in the eye of a storm, where everything around you is raging yet you feel the warmth of His peace enveloping you.*)

Zechariah 4:6—"Not by might nor by power, but by My Spirit," says the Lord of hosts.

Malachi 3:6—I am the Lord, I do not change.

Matthew 1:1–16—*I won't include the entire passage, but I want to point out some people in the genealogy of Jesus because truly this genealogy is a story of God's grace. Many of these people turned from God's way and sinned against Him in some monumental ways. For example, Abraham took Hagar to try to fulfil God's promise that he would have a son. Jacob stole Esau's birthright and blessing. Judah took his son's widow Tamar, thinking she was a prostitute, and together they had Perez, whom God specifically named. Rahab was a prostitute who had Boaz (a foretelling of Jesus as the kinsman-redeemer). Ruth was a pagan who decided to follow the God of Israel (a foretelling of Gentiles being grafted into the promises of God). King David was an adulterer and a murderer. On and on the list goes, yet all these sinful people brought forth Mary, the mother of Jesus, the Savior of the world.)*

Matthew 6:33—Seek first the kingdom of God and His righteousness, and all these things shall be added to you.

Matthew 7:7, 11—Ask, and it will be given to you; seek, and you will find; knock, and it will be opened to you. . . . How much more will your Father who is in heaven give good things to those who ask?

Matthew 8:16—He cast out the spirits with a word.

Matthew 8:26—Then He arose and rebuked the winds and the sea, and there was a great calm.

Matthew 7:25—The rain descended, the floods came, and the winds blew and beat on that house; and it did not fall, for it was founded on the rock. (*The rock is Jesus!*)

Matthew 10:30–31—The very hairs of your head are numbered. Do not fear therefore; you are of more value than many sparrows.

Matthew 10:39—He who finds his life will lose it, and he who loses his life for my sake will find it.

Matthew 11:28—Come to Me, all you who labor and are heavy laden, and I will give you rest.

Matthew 12:20—A bruised reed He will not break, and a smoldering wick He will not snuff out, till He has brought justice through to victory (NIV).

Matthew 18:12—If a man has a hundred sheep, and one of them goes astray, does he not leave the ninety-nine and go to the mountains to seek the one that is straying?

Matthew 18:18—Whatever you bind on earth will be bound in heaven, and whatever you loose on earth will be loosed in heaven.

Matthew 18:19–20—If two of you agree on earth concerning anything that they ask, it will be done for them by my Father in Heaven. For where two or three are gathered in My name, I am there in the midst of them.

Matthew 19:26—With men this is impossible, but with God all things are possible.

Mark 9:23—Jesus said to him, "If you can believe, all things are possible to him who believes."

Mark 10:27—Jesus looked at them and said, "With men it is impossible, but not with God; for with God all things are possible."

Mark 11:24—Whatever things you ask when you pray, believe that you receive them, and you will have them.

Luke 1:37—With God nothing will be impossible.

Luke 1:50—His mercy is on those who fear Him from generation to generation.

Luke 9:56—The Son of Man did not come to destroy men's lives but to save them.

Luke 10:19—Behold, I give you the authority . . . over all the power of the enemy, and nothing shall by any means hurt you.

Luke 11:9—I say to you, ask, and it will be given to you; seek, and you will find; knock, and it will be opened to you.

Luke 12:7—The very hairs of your head are numbered. Do not fear therefore; you are of more value than many sparrows.

Luke 12:31—Seek the kingdom of God, and all these things shall be added to you.

Luke 18:27—The things which are impossible with men are possible with God.

John 3:16–17—For God so loved the world that He gave His only begotten Son, that whoever believes in Him should not perish but have everlasting life. For God did not send His Son into the world to condemn the world, but that the world through Him might be saved.

John 6:40—This is the will of Him who sent me, that everyone who sees the Son and believes in Him may have everlasting life. (*This is why I knew my prayers for Minnie's salvation were also God's will. His will is that all will be saved, so I could pray in confidence, knowing that for anything I ask according to His will, it will be done!*)

John 8:36—If the Son of Man makes you free, you shall be free indeed. (*Jesus set Minnie free!*)

John 10:10—The thief does not come except to steal, and to kill, and to destroy. I have come that they may have life, and that they may have it more abundantly.

John 10:27–30—My sheep hear My voice, and I know them, and they follow Me. And I give them eternal life, and they shall never perish; neither shall anyone snatch them out of my hand. My Father, who has given them to Me, is greater than all; and no one is able to snatch them out of My Father's hand. I and My

Father are one. (*This passage is especially important to me, to those of us whose prodigal children had at one point given their hearts to Jesus. He promised that nothing can snatch them from Him, and that includes their own defiance.*)

John 11:25—Jesus said to her, "I am the resurrection and the life. He who believes in Me, though he may die, he shall live." *Praise God!*

John 14:13–14—Whatever you ask in My name, that I will do, that the Father may be glorified in the Son. If you ask anything in My name, I will do it.

John 14:27—Peace I leave with you, My peace I give to you; not as the world gives do I give to you. Let not your heart be troubled, neither let it be afraid.

John 16:33—These things I have spoken to you, that in Me you may have peace. In the world you will have tribulation; but be of good cheer, I have overcome the world.

John 17:12—Those whom You gave Me I have kept; and none of them is lost except the son of perdition, that the Scripture might be fulfilled. (*Yes! God gave Minnie to Jesus, and not one of those He has been given is lost!*)

Acts 2:21—Whoever calls on the name of the Lord shall be saved.

Acts 16:31—Believe on the Lord Jesus Christ, and you will be saved, you and your household.

Acts 17:26–27—[He] has determined their preappointed times and the boundaries of their dwellings, so that they should seek the Lord, in the hope that they might grope for Him and find Him, though He is not far from each one of us. (*How great is our God, to place us each in the time and place where we would individually be most likely to find Him and come to Him!*)

Romans 2:4—The goodness of God leads you to repentance.

Romans 4:3, 18, 20—Abraham believed God, and it was accounted to him for righteousness (*Abraham was considered righteous not by the law, which had not yet been given, but simply by believing God.*) . . . who, contrary to hope, in hope believed. . . . He did not waver at the promise of God through unbelief, but was strengthened in faith, giving glory to God, and being fully convinced that what He had promised He was also able to perform. (*When there was nothing his eye could see that would give him hope, still he hoped—because his hope was based on God's character*).

Romans 5:2–5—Therefore, having been justified by faith, we have peace with God through our Lord Jesus Christ, through whom also we have access by faith into this grace in which we stand, and rejoice in hope of the glory of God. And not only that, but we also glory in tribulations, knowing that tribulation produces perseverance; and perseverance, character; and character, hope. Now hope does not disappoint, because the love of God has been poured out in our hearts by the Holy Spirit who was given to us.

Romans 5:20—Where sin abounded, grace abounded much more.

Romans 6:23—The wages of sin is death, but the gift of God is eternal life in Christ Jesus our Lord.

Romans 7:24–25—O wretched man that I am! Who will deliver me from this body of death? I thank God—through Jesus Christ our Lord!

Romans 8:18—I consider that the sufferings of this present time are not worthy to be compared with the glory which shall be revealed in us.

Romans 8:26—The Spirit also helps in our weaknesses. For we do not know what we should pray for as we ought, but the Spirit Himself makes intercession for us with groanings which cannot be uttered.

Romans 8:28—We know that all things work together for good to those who love God, to those who are the called according to His purpose. (*I once heard someone explain it like this: there is a cooking show in which the contestants are given a bunch of random and sometimes appalling ingredients, and they have to whip up a gourmet masterpiece out of them all. This is like what God does in our lives. He takes all the unpleasant, offensive, dreadful, ugly, and seemingly accidental or arbitrary things in our lives and works them into a beautiful show-stopping masterpiece.*)

Romans 8:35, 37–39—Who shall separate us from the love of Christ? Shall tribulation, or distress, or persecution, or famine, or nakedness, or peril, or sword? . . . Yet in all these things we are more than conquerors through Him who loved us. For I am persuaded that neither death nor life, nor angels nor principalities nor powers, nor things present nor things to come, nor height nor depth, nor any other created thing, shall be able to separate us from the love of God which is in Christ Jesus our Lord. (*Oh, how amazing it is to be loved by God! The other day when I was having another low moment of grief, I opened up my little leather journal right to this page, and it was like God reminding me again that* nothing, *not even Minnie's own bad decisions and disobedience, could separate her from His love.*)

Romans 10:9–10, 13—If you confess with your mouth the Lord Jesus and believe in your heart that God has raised Him from the dead, you will be saved. For with the heart one believes unto righteousness, and with the mouth confession is made unto salvation. . . . For "whoever calls on the name of the Lord shall be saved."

Romans 12:12—Rejoicing in hope, patient in tribulation, continuing steadfastly in prayer.

Romans 15:13—Now may the God of hope fill you with all joy and peace in believing, that you may abound in hope by the power of the Holy Spirit.

I Corinthians 15:26, 54, 57—The last enemy that will be destroyed is death. . . . Death is swallowed up in victory. . . . But thanks be to God, who gives us the victory through our Lord Jesus Christ.

2 Corinthians 1:3–4—Blessed be the God and Father of our Lord Jesus Christ, the Father of mercies and God of all comfort, who comforts us in all our tribulation, that we may be able to comfort those who are in any trouble, with the comfort with which we ourselves are comforted by God.

2 Corinthians 1:20—All the promises of God in Him are Yes, and in Him Amen, to the glory of God through us.

2 Corinthians 2:14—Now thanks be to God who always leads us in triumph in Christ, and through us diffuses the fragrance of His knowledge in every place.

2 Corinthians 4:8–9, 17—We are hard-pressed on every side, yet not crushed; we are perplexed, but not in despair; persecuted, but not forsaken; struck down, but not destroyed. . . . For our light affliction, which is but for a moment, is working for us a far more exceeding and eternal weight of glory,

2 Corinthians 5:7—We walk by faith, not by sight.

2 Corinthians 5:17—If anyone is in Christ, he is a new creation; old things have passed away; behold, all things have become new.

2 Corinthians 6:2—In an acceptable time I have heard you, and in the day of salvation I have helped you.

2 Corinthians 9:8—God is able to make all grace abound toward you, that you, always having all sufficiency in all things, may have an abundance for every good work.

2 Corinthians 9:15—Thanks be to God for His indescribable gift!

2 Corinthians 10:4–5—The weapons of our warfare are not carnal but mighty in God for pulling down strongholds, casting down arguments and every high thing that exalts itself against the knowledge of God, bringing every thought into captivity to the obedience of Christ,

2 Corinthians 12:9—He said to me, "My grace is sufficient for you, for My strength is made perfect in weakness."

Galatians 6:9—Let us not grow weary while doing good, for in due season we shall reap if we do not lose heart.

Ephesians 2:4–9—God, who is rich in mercy, because of His great love with which He loved us, even when we were dead in trespasses, made us alive together with Christ (by grace you have been saved), and raised us up together, and made us sit together in the heavenly places in Christ Jesus, that in the ages to come He might show the exceeding riches of His grace in His kindness toward us in Christ Jesus. For by grace you have been saved through faith, and that not of yourselves; it is the gift of God, not of works, lest anyone should boast. (*His grace truly is amazing. We cannot earn it. There is nothing we could ever do to deserve it. His grace covered all of Minnie's failings, because she had given her heart to Him many years ago. If salvation were by works, none of us could ever be saved.*)

Ephesians 3:18–19—[That you] may be able to comprehend with all the saints what is the width and length and depth and height—to know the love of Christ which passes knowledge; that you may be filled with all the fullness of God. (*We will never be able to comprehend His great love for us until we are standing before Him enveloped in His love.*)

Ephesians 3:20–21—Now to Him who is able to do exceedingly abundantly above all that we ask or think, according to the power that works in us, to Him be glory in the church by Christ Jesus to all generations, forever and ever. Amen.

Ephesians 6:10–13—Finally, my brethren, be strong in the Lord and in the power of His might. Put on the whole armor of God, that you may be able to stand against the wiles of the devil. For we do not wrestle against flesh and blood, but against principalities, against powers, against the rulers of the darkness of this age, against spiritual hosts of wickedness in the heavenly places. Therefore take up the whole armor of God, that you may be able to withstand in the evil day, and having done all, to stand.

Philippians 1:6—Being confident of this very thing, that He who has begun a good work in you will complete it until the day of Jesus Christ.

Philippians 2:13—It is God who works in you both to will and to do for His good pleasure.

Philippians 3:12–14—Not that I have already attained, or am already perfected; but I press on, that I may lay hold of that for which Christ Jesus has also laid hold of me. Brethren, I do not count myself to have apprehended; but one thing I do, forgetting those things which are behind and reaching forward to those things which are ahead, I press toward the goal for the prize of the upward call of God in Christ Jesus.

Philippians 3:20–21—Our citizenship is in heaven, from which we also eagerly wait for the Savior, the Lord Jesus Christ, who will transform our lowly body that it may be conformed to His glorious body. (*This is the promise for our eternal future!*)

Philippians 4:4, 6–7—Rejoice in the Lord always. Again I will say, rejoice! Be anxious for nothing, but in everything by prayer and supplication, with thanksgiving, let your requests be made known to God; and the peace of God, which surpasses all understanding, will guard your hearts and minds through Christ Jesus. (*I can tell you from experience that this promise is true! The true peace I have felt through this fiery trial genuinely surpasses all understanding and can be only from God. There is no way I could ever even take another step without Jesus. I've said it every single day since Minnie passed, "How can anyone go through life without Him?"*)

Philippians 4:13—I can do all things through Christ who strengthens me.

Philippians 4:19—My God shall supply all your need according to His riches in glory by Christ Jesus.

Colossians 1:13–14—He has delivered us from the power of darkness and conveyed us into the kingdom of the Son of His love, in whom we have redemption through His blood, the forgiveness of sins.

Colossians 2:13–14—He has made alive together with Him, having forgiven you all trespasses, having wiped out the handwriting of requirements that was against us, which was contrary to us. And He has taken it out of the way, having nailed it to the cross. (*Again, being good, keeping the law, and works cannot save. It is the cross of Jesus Christ alone, His grace, that gives us eternal life.*)

Colossians 3:15—Let the peace of God rule in your hearts.

Colossians 4:2—Continue earnestly in prayer, bring vigilant in it with thanksgiving.

1 Thessalonians 4:13–14—I do not want you to be ignorant, brethren, concerning those who have fallen asleep, lest you sorrow as others who have no hope. For if we believe that Jesus died and rose again, even so God will bring with Him those who sleep in Jesus. (*I added this emphasis because this makes all the difference. Amen! We do not sorrow as those who have no hope! I will see my Minnie again. Death is not the end, and we will be together again.*)

1 Thessalonians 5:9–10—God did not appoint us to wrath, but to obtain salvation through our Lord Jesus Christ, who died for us, that whether we wake or sleep, we should live together with Him. (*God does not want any of us to go to hell, but He died so we can all be saved. However, it is our choice whether to accept His salvation or not. He does not send anyone to hell— a person's rejection of Jesus sends him or her to hell.*)

1 Timothy 6:12—Fight the good fight of faith, lay hold on eternal life, to which you were also called and have confessed the good confession in the presence of many witnesses.

2 Timothy 1:7—God has not given us a spirit of fear, but of power and of love and of a sound mind.

2 Timothy 3:15—From childhood you have known the Holy Scriptures, which are able to make you wise for salvation through faith which is in Christ Jesus. (*This goes along with Proverbs 22:6: "Train up a child in the way he should go, and when he is old he will not depart from it." Both of these verses speak to parents. As it is our job to teach our children the Word of God, so, even if they stray, they know the way to salvation through Christ Jesus. This is*

an amazing promise for all parents of prodigal children. If we've done our part, as God commanded, He will do His part and fulfill His promises. This verse also goes along with the next two verses . . . keep reading.)

2 Timothy 3:16–17—All Scripture is given by inspiration of God, and is profitable for doctrine, for reproof, for correction, for instruction in righteousness, that the man of God may be complete, thoroughly equipped for every good work. (*This is why it is of vital importance not only to study and know Scripture but also to teach it to our children.*)

2 Timothy 4:7–8—I have fought the good fight, I have finished the race, I have kept the faith. Finally, there is laid up for me the crown of righteousness, which the Lord, the righteous Judge, will give to me on that Day, and not to me only but also to all who have loved His appearing. (*Even on days I don't feel like fighting, He keeps me in the race and moving toward my crown. I long for that day!*)

Titus 3:4–7—When the kindness and the love of God our Savior toward man appeared, not by works of righteousness which we have done, but according to His mercy He saved us, through the washing of regeneration and renewing of the Holy Spirit, whom He poured out on us abundantly through Jesus Christ our Savior, that having been justified by His grace we should become heirs according to the hope of eternal life. (*In a word, grace. There is nothing we could have done and nothing we can do, but it is only by His grace that we receive eternal life.*)

Hebrews 4:15–16—We do not have a High Priest who cannot sympathize with our weaknesses, but was in all points tempted as we are, yet without sin. Let us therefore come boldly to the throne of grace, that we may obtain mercy and find grace to help in time of need. (*This is for me! Jesus says to me, "Come," and I can go to Him boldly, and there He gives mercy and grace for everything I need.*)

Hebrews 6:19—This hope we have as an anchor of the soul, both sure and steadfast, and which enters the Presence behind the veil. (*So many have asked me how I can be so strong. If they only know just how weak I am. My strength is* only *because my soul is anchored to the rock, and He keeps me from tossing this way and that through even the most raging storm. My prayer is that those around me see that He has made all the difference.*)

Hebrews 7:25—He is also able to save to the uttermost those who come to God through Him, since He always lives to make intercession for them. (Uttermost *means the final, the ultimate, the last; He can save down to the very last sin. There is nothing we can do that He cannot save us from. But He doesn't stop there! He is forever before the Father actually interceding for us! I am totally humbled; undone!*)

Hebrews 10:23—Let us hold fast the confession of our hope without wavering, *for He who promised is* faithful. (*The emphasis here is mine, because if you get nothing else from thing entire book, I want you to get the* fact *that He is faithful!*)

Hebrews 11:1, 6—Now faith is the substance of things hoped for, the evidence of things not seen. . . . But without faith it is impossible to please Him, for he who comes to God must believe that He is, and that He is a rewarder of those who diligently seek Him.

Hebrews 12:1–2—We also, since we are surrounded by so great a cloud of witnesses, let us lay aside every weight, and the sin which so easily ensnares us, and let us run with endurance the race that is set before us, looking unto Jesus, the author and finisher of our faith, who for the joy that was set before Him endured the cross, despising the shame, and has sat down at the right hand of the throne of God. (*First let me say that this was the exact passage I read the morning Minnie passed, before I ever even knew she was gone. Remember Greg Laurie's Book Hope for Hurting Hearts; he points out that the "therefore" refers back to those heroes of faith mentioned in the previous chapter, those who have passed on before us. So what this means is that those who have gone to heaven are watching us and cheering us on! That means my Minnie, who I cheered on and encouraged for eighteen years, while I was reading this passage that November morning was already in heaven cheering me on, and I didn't even know it yet. Wow!*)

Hebrews 12:11—Now no chastening seems to be joyful for the present, but painful; nevertheless, afterward it yields the peaceable fruit of righteousness to those who have been trained by it. (*No one likes discipline; however, God prunes us so we will yield the best and sweetest fruit. My neighbor is a master gardener and every winter he prunes his blackberry bushes down to what looks like dead, worthless stumps. However, year after year those blackberries come in huge, beautiful, and sweet!*)

Hebrews 13:8—Jesus Christ is the same yesterday, today, and forever. (*This means that if He kept all of His promises to those mentioned in the Bible, He will keep His promises to us!*)

James 3:13—Mercy triumphs over judgement. (*This!*)

James 4:8, 10—Draw near to God and He will draw near to you. . . . Humble yourselves in the sight of the Lord, and He will lift you up.

James 5:16—The effective, fervent prayer of a righteous man avails much.

1 Peter 1:3–4 —Blessed be the God and Father of our Lord Jesus Christ, who according to His abundant mercy has begotten us again to a living hope through the resurrection of Jesus Christ from the dead, to an inheritance incorruptible and undefiled and that does not fade away, reserved in heaven for you (*His abundant mercy!*).

1 Peter 1:8–9—Though now you do not see Him, yet believing, you rejoice with joy inexpressible and full of glory, receiving the end of your faith—the salvation of your souls. (*Inexpressible joy comes from the fact that my soul is saved and that I will see Minnie again. This life is short, and our problems are momentary, but eternity is forever so I anxiously wait for that day.*)

1 Peter 1:18–19; 2:24—Knowing that you were not redeemed with corruptible things, like silver or gold, from your aimless conduct received by tradition from your fathers, but with the precious blood of Christ, as of a lamb without blemish and without spot (*Gold, silver, idols, works—nothing else can save but the precious blood Jesus willingly spilled for us.*) . . . who Himself bore our sins in His own body on the tree, that we, having died to sins, might live for righteousness—by whose stripes you were healed.

1 Peter 5:6–7—Humble yourselves under the mighty hand of God, that He may exalt you in due time, casting all your care upon Him, for He cares for you.

1 Peter 5:10—May the God of all grace, who called us to His eternal glory through Christ Jesus, after you have suffered a while, perfect, establish, strengthen, and settle you. (*Yes, sometimes we have to suffer, but His grace is working to "perfect, establish, strengthen, and settle" us. What a beautiful reminder that He is always working in our lives, even in our suffering!*)

2 Peter 3:9, 15—The Lord is not slack concerning His promise, as some count slackness, but is longsuffering toward us, not willing that any should perish but that all should come to repentance. . . . and consider that the longsuffering of our Lord is salvation. (*This again speaks of God's mercy. He is longsuffering—beyond patient—waiting for the lost to come to Him.*).

1 John 1:9—If we confess our sins He is faithful and just to forgive us our sins and to cleanse us from all unrighteousness.

1 John 2:1–2—If anyone sins, we have an Advocate with the Father, Jesus Christ the righteous. And He Himself is the propitiation for our sins. (*Propitiation means "satisfying the wrath of God against sin." Can you even comprehend that Jesus, who is God, gave Himself as an offering to the Father so His wrath doesn't fall on us? He is our advocate, or lawyer. This is as if you were on trial and received the death penalty, and your own lawyer decided to die in your place so you can go free because it satisfies the judge's punishment toward you. It doesn't make any sense to us, but He loves us that much.*)

1 John 3:1—Behold what manner of love the Father has bestowed on us, that we should be called children of God!

1 John 4:4—He who is in you is greater than he who is in the world.

1 John 4:9—In this is love, not that we loved God, but that He loved. us and sent His Son to be the propitiation for our sins.

1 John 5:14—Now this is the confidence that we have in Him, that if we ask anything according to His will, He hears us.

Let's look at some awe-inspiring and marvelous future promises for those of us who believe in the Lord Jesus Christ:

Revelation 2:7—To him who overcomes I will give to eat from the tree of life, which is in the midst of the Paradise of God. (*When*

Adam and Eve sinned, God removed them from the Garden of Eden and removed their access to the tree of life. This was not just a punishment; no, it was also great mercy. If they ate of the tree of life after they sinned, they would have had to live in eternal separation from God. Death was the curse of sin; however, it is through death that the curse of sin is finally broken because we can once again be with God in paradise and eat of the tree of life and live for eternity in perfect communion with Him.)

Revelation 3:10–12—Because you have kept My command to persevere, I also will keep you from the hour of trial which shall come upon the whole world, to test those who dwell on the earth. Behold, I am coming quickly! Hold fast what you have, that no one may take your crown. He who overcomes, I will make him a pillar in the temple of My God, and he shall go out no more. I will write on him the name of My God and the name of the city of My God, the New Jerusalem, which comes down out of heaven from My God. And *I will write on him* My new name. *(Emphasis added. The hour of trial coming on the whole world is the tribulation. This promise right here says he will keep us from that hour of trial! This is called the rapture of the church. Not to get too thick into prophecy here, but the church is not mentioned again after this chapter. Why? Because the church will be taken out of here before the wrath of God hits the rest of the world. And all the prophetic signs are converging, which means the rapture is near . . . and I will see my Jesus and my Minnie again very soon! This is the most comforting thing to me, which I dwell on all day long.)*

Revelation 3:21—To him who overcomes I will grant to sit with Me on My throne, as I also overcame and sat down with My Father on His throne. *(Read this again—Jesus is going to invite us to sit on* His *throne! Oh, such love! How could we ever comprehend it? All we can do is try to imagine, and then just try to breathe Him in as we bask in His presence.)*

Revelation 21:4—God will wipe away every tear from their eyes; there shall be no more death, nor sorrow, nor crying. There shall be no more pain, for the former things have passed away." (*There is nothing more I could ever ask for or imagine.*)

Revelation 22:20—"Surely I am coming quickly." Amen. Even so, come, Lord Jesus! (*And to this I say, "Yes! Amen!"*)

EPILOGUE

Today was Minnie's nineteenth birthday. I went to place flowers on her grave, and I thought I would pick up the flowers from a vendor on the side of the road. I stopped at the first one I came to and asked her for red roses, Minnie's favorite. She picked up a few bundles and I decided on one of them. As she handed them to me, there they were—big yellow butterflies all over the blue plastic wrapping surrounding the flowers. God's lovingkindness and tender mercies never stop running after me.

WORKS CITED

Cowman, L. B., et al. *Streams in the Desert*. Grand Rapids, MI: Zondervan Publishing House, 1997.

Elliot, Elisabeth, and Joni Eareckson Tada. *Suffering Is Never for Nothing*. Nashville: B & H Publishing Group, 2019.

GotQuestions.org. January 4, 2022. www.gotquestions.org/prayer-fasting.html.

Hixson, J. B. "Dr. Hixson Answers Your Questions," no. 1026, September 27, 2024, audio podcast episode. In *NBW Ministries Podcast*. NBW Ministries—Home, notbyworks.org

Hibbs, Jack. *What Are You Waiting For?* Sermon, part 3, September 24, 2023. Calvary Chapel, Chino Hills, CA.

------. "Will Backsliders Be Raptured?" no. 198, February 15, 2024, audio podcast episode. In *Jack Hibbs Podcast*. https://jackhibbs.com

Hutchcraft, Ron. *Hope When Your Heart Is Breaking.* Eugene, OR: Harvest House Publishers, 2021.

Laurie, Greg. *Hope for Hurting Hearts.* Dana Point, CA: Kerygma Publishing, 2008.

Lewis, C. S. *The Problem of Pain.* London: Harper Collins, 2012.

Rogers, Matt. (2021, April 14). Teri Rogers (part 2), no. 115, April 14, 2021, audio podcast episode. In *Level Up with Matt Rogers.*

Spurgeon, Charles H. *Faith's Checkbook.* Updated version. Abbotsford, WI: Aneko Press, 2020.

Walsh, Jenny. "A Mother's Heart on Praying for Her Prodigal Son." *Revive Our Hearts*, August 6, 2019, www.reviveourhearts.com/blog/mothers-heart-praying-her-prodigal-son/. Accessed May 31, 2024.

Weimer, Heidi R. *How Do I Kiss You?* La Jolla, CA: Smart Kids Publishing, 2007.

www.ingramcontent.com/pod-product-compliance
Lightning Source LLC
Chambersburg PA
CBHW060517100426
42743CB00009B/1351